Railroad Collisions, A Deadly Story of Mismanaged Risk

Railroad Collisions, A Deadly Story of Mismanaged Risk

. . .

George Swimmer

ISBN: 1517106338
ISBN 13: 9781517106331
Library of Congress Control Number: 2015914521
CreateSpace Independent Publishing Platform
North Charleston, South Carolina

TO CARRIE,

The beauty of a sunny day, the joy of seeing children play

The water ripples to the shore, it is you, my love, that I adore

The pureness of the morning air, the thought of knowing that you care

The bird that circles from above, it is you, my darling, that I love

The trees alive with colors of gold, the sweetest love that can be told

The rays of sun on the water shine, it is you that makes my life so fine

Love, George

Contents

Prologue

. . .

For every action, there is an equal and opposite reaction.

—SIR ISAAC NEWTON

A HANDFUL OF PEOPLE SEEM to remember in detail almost every day of their lives. Personally, I can only remember some details of some days. Some specific events I recall with clarity. Many are joyful, and some are not.

Tuesday, September 26, 1989, started out like most workdays. I only have memories of very brief parts of this day. But those moments changed the direction of my life. Going back in time I will weave a story you may find difficult to believe. Truth is often stranger than fiction.

Cass Avenue, in Chicago's suburb of Darien, Illinois, is a major north-south street. It was early evening and traffic, as usual, was very heavy. I was stopped in the left lane and waiting for oncoming traffic to clear in order to make a left turn into my office parking lot. As I looked into my rearview mirror, I knew the approaching driver was about to slam into the back of my car. That look of fright in the driver's eyes remains unforgettable. She was just a second or two away when she realized she would not be able to stop. The small children in her car may have distracted her. Fortunately, she and her children were not hurt.

After the collision, I was dazed, confused, and my back and neck hurt. Soon after, a young Darien police officer arrived. He immediately placed his hands around my neck, telling me he wanted to stabilize my neck in case there were spinal injuries. A passerby might have thought the officer was choking me. I never thanked him, so now is my chance. Thank you for making that special effort.

Ambulance paramedics briefly treated me at the scene and then placed me in the ambulance and rushed me to nearby Hinsdale Hospital. Loud voices were blaring from the ambulance's radio speakers. The voices belonged to paramedics at a nearby railroad crossing accident as they talked to who I believe were emergency room doctors.

As I later learned, the Monroe Street (DOT/AAR 079526W) railroad crossing in Hinsdale, Illinois, was the scene of this serious train-versus-pedestrian accident. The young boy, eleven-year-old Jonathan Goers, had been struck by a Metra/BNSF train traveling at about twenty mph.

Monroe Street Crossing, Hinsdale, Illinois

While paramedics treated young Jonathan at the scene at the Monroe Street crossing, other paramedics were treating me in the back of the ambulance as it sped to the hospital. Paramedics at the other scene indicated on the radio that the injured person's arms were flailing wildly, and there was talk of airlifting him to a trauma center hospital. It was obvious the boy had sustained serious injuries. The decision was made to chemically render him unconscious. The few minutes it took to rush me to the hospital brought out emotions I still feel to this day.

Until that day, Jonathan was an active boy who played on the Monroe School soccer team. His life—and the lives of his family members—would change forever that day. He had waited at the busy train crossing for one train to pass before starting to cross the tracks. A Metra/BNSF train coming from the opposite direction struck him. He was thrown thirty feet.

Today, more than twenty years later, Jonathan lives in a permanent care facility. He is fed by a tube and has daily seizures. He has the mental functioning of an infant. My injuries were superficial, and I was sent home that night to recover.

Ellie and Dick Goers are Jonathan's parents. I met them some years after the accident and now know them well. Jonathan is often in my thoughts. This book is for him. He inspired me more than he will ever know.

On March 2, 1994, a seventeen-year-old driver made an irreversible error in judgment. He raced a westbound moving train for several blocks, and then went around downed railroad crossing gates at that same Monroe Street crossing in Hinsdale where young Jonathan Goers had been hurt almost five years earlier.

Lauren Wilson, fourteen, was the only passenger. She was killed, and the driver was seriously injured when the car was struck by a Metra/BNSF commuter train traveling at about sixty-nine mph.

Lauren was a student at Hinsdale Central High School. She was president of the freshman class, a member of the Future Problem Solvers Club, and active in theater. At the time of the collision, she was being driven to a rehearsal of the *Phantom Tollbooth*, a play in which she was appearing.

Over the years, Lauren's father, Dr. Lanny Wilson and I have become friends. Ever since that tragic day, Dr. Wilson has spent countless hours working to prevent other tragedies on the railroad tracks.

Shortly after Lauren's death, the DuPage Railroad Safety Council (DRSC), a citizen advocate group, was formed. DuPage County, where I live, is immediately west of Chicago's Cook County. Those of us who are members of the council are passionately and actively involved in improving rail safety. For many members of the DRSC, our knowledge about railroading and railroad safety issues has been acquired through many years of involvement with this group. Under the chairmanship of Dr. Wilson, the council has been blessed by the insights and knowledge of a membership including locomotive engineers, railroad officials and safety experts, police officers, government officials, elected officials, Federal Railroad Administration employees, citizen advocates, family members of accident victims, a judge, and many more.

It is important to emphasize that this book doesn't reflect the thoughts, ideas, or conclusions of the DRSC or any of its members except my own. Indeed, many DRSC members will have opposite viewpoints. Even so, we all give of our time and work to make railroad tracks safer for everyone.

Steve Laffey is widely known and highly respected in rail safety circles for his knowledge of railroading and his passion to improve safety. He is employed by the Illinois Commerce Commission as a railroad safety specialist, is a volunteer member of the Board of

Directors for the DuPage Railroad Safety Council, and is chair of the Transportation Research Board committee on highway/rail grade crossings. Prior to submitting what I thought would be close to a final version, I asked Mr. Laffey if he would take a look at the manuscript and give me his thoughts. After some time, I received back his edited version, which I know took many hours, and probably many days, for him to complete. He made corrections, gave me his thoughts, and provided information that I had not previously been aware of. Thank you, Steve Laffey, for your candor, wisdom, and helpfulness.

When I thought the book was almost complete but still needed a final edit I reached out to my friend Daniel Paul for help. Mr. Paul is a young professional who graduated from the University of Alabama with an MBA. His undergraduate major was Japanese. His comments, suggestions, and many hours of editing can only add to a better manuscript. When he said that he thought the book was a good and informative read, I felt exceptionally gratified. I respect his opinion so very much. Thank you, Daniel Paul.

In early May 2015 the book was finally finished, or at least I thought so, and I gave or mailed out twenty copies. Some to government officials, some to the media, some to the authors cited for articles they had written that I used in this book to support one argument or another, one to my dear friends Jim and Beverly Rogers, and one to a locomotive engineer Steve Frankowiak.

Jim and Beverly Rogers are my dear friends. Jim and I go back to our high school days at Amundsen in Chicago, and then almost six years together in the same Marine Corps unit. I had been telling Jim about my writing of a book for years. I wanted him to have one of the first copies. Little did I know at the time that his wonderful wife Bev was a retired proofreader. Thanks, Bev, for spending so much time proofreading the book.

Steve Frankowiak is a locomotive engineer whom I had met some time ago at the DuPage Railroad Safety Council. I hadn't seen Steve at a meeting for several years. He was now retired and living in Arizona. I asked him if he would read the book and give me his comments. He eagerly volunteered, and I mailed him a copy.

Before retiring, Steve had thirty-eight years of railroading experience, starting with the Chicago and North Western Transportation Company (C&NW), which eventually merged into the Union Pacific (UP). In 1976 he became a brakeman for two years, then a fireman for two years, and then a locomotive engineer for over thirty years. He had worked both the freight and commuter services, and acted as a legislative representative for his union, the Brotherhood of Locomotive Engineers and Trainmen (BLET). He not only wrote his editing comments in the book, but I had the opportunity to sit with him for two hours over breakfast and talk railroading. He was visiting his son who lives in a Chicago suburb. His insights have made this book more meaningful, and I thank him.

There is one section of the book that talks about trains passing through commuter stations on the Chicago-area BNSF line when there is a commuter train either in the station or just exiting the station. When we met, Steve stated "[this practice] defies common sense." I think about that comment often and would like to add that there are other railroading practices described in this book that defies common sense.

This book was made possible through my life experiences, the help of many with whom I have met over the years, and the many investigative reporters who have written articles that I used to support one argument or another.

There was a series of articles that I came across after sending out the first twenty copies. Walt Bogdanich of the *New York Times* won a Pulitzer Prize for a series of detailed investigative articles on railroad accidents and safety that he wrote in 2004. It's an amazing and brilliant investigative series.

Prior to that ambulance ride in 1989, the only thing I knew about railroading was that when the gates go down, a train is approaching.

In the children's book *The Little Engine That Could*, by Watty Piper, the little locomotive engine struggled to get up that hill and finally made it to the top. Over the years, I have investigated many railroad accidents involving trains versus other trains, cars and trucks, pedestrians and trespassers, have written many articles and opinion/editorial pieces, testified in front of governmental groups, and helped bring about change—both locally and nationally—that significantly improved rail safety.

The knowledge that I have helped improve rail safety gives me tremendous satisfaction. But that satisfaction is dampened by my disappointment in how long it takes to make positive and meaningful change. This book is controversial and may provoke a reaction. Hopefully, that reaction will result in positive changes in railroad safety.

The purpose of this book is threefold: to reduce injuries and save lives, to tell a story in a way that you might find not only interesting but also motivational, and lastly to honor and recognize some very special people.

After I became involved in railroad safety issues, I took a graduate level writing course at Governors State University in University Park, Illinois. The goal of the course was to show how to, in writing, present an argument and then support that argument in a meaningful way. If this book reaches any level of success, I certainly give credit to the amazing teacher who taught the course.

In this book, I present many different arguments and claims that will be controversial, with each supported by various forms of evidence, facts, or reasons. Although the chapters are somewhat grouped together to support a specific argument, it is not possible to do so all of the time. Some chapters, although not grouped together, will illustrate reasons that support several different arguments or claims made in other parts of the book.

For example, I claim that the Federal Railroad Administration (FRA) is timid in dealing with the railroads. Several chapters support this. The chapter "Accident Investigation" reflects how many years it took for the railroad locomotives to simply turn on their triangular lighting pattern. Federal regulations only "recommended" that they be turned on for the five years prior to the required turn-on date. I include a series of chapters that relate to second-train incidents near commuter train stations. In one chapter, I relate a conversation I had many years ago, with an FRA official, in which he had been alerted by locomotive engineers about the dangers of second-train accidents along the Burlington Northern Santa Fe (BNSF) line near commuter stations. Many years have now passed, and the same dangers still exist. In my opinion, the BNSF poorly manages risk near commuter stations in the Chicago and suburban area, has done so for years, and is doing little to make their operations safer.

In the chapter "Signal Problems," I address a very serious problem in which a specific signal-system relay at times did not work correctly, The FRA felt it so serious that it issued a safety advisory in the year 2000 alerting the railroads of the problem, but then only "recommended" that the 2,000,000 or so relays be inspected and repaired if needed. I then point out how, time after time, the FRA has warned specific railroads that they are operating without a culture of safety.

A series of chapters tell of malfunctioning active warning devices, gates, signals and bells, at highway railroad grade crossings that have resulted in railroad versus vehicle collisions. The chapters are "Tragedy on the Tracks," "Honoring Our Veterans," "The City of

New Orleans," and "Katie Ann Lunn." I make the argument that a redundant, independent warning system is needed at highway grade crossings, and that the sounding of the train horn alone by the locomotive engineer is inadequate.

Five chapters focus on when trains either derailed or collided head on with other trains, and the National Transportation Safety Board (NTSB) indicated that, in each accident, the most significant contributing factor was a missed signal aspect by the locomotive engineer. It is my opinion that the signals malfunctioned and gave false clears, or incorrect signal aspects, and the engineers read them as indicated, which led to the accident or derailment.

It is also my opinion that the NTSB did little, if any, meaningful pattern analyses, that they gave little credibility to testimony from eyewitness after eyewitness, and that their conclusions are simply wrong. In fact, I believe their accident reports that relate to these specific events have done more harm than good. If there are bad signals out there—and the FRA has already told us there are—then the powerful NTSB accident reports led us in a completely different direction.

Meaningful statistics are the lifeblood of any good safety system. They allow us to see where problems exist, the magnitude of these problems, why they exist, and they lead us to finding solutions that better manage risk. In the chapter "Incident Reporting: Out of Sight, Out of Mind," there is example after example where railroads file flawed accident reports. The railroads are required to prepare and file these accident reports with the FRA, and the FRA relies on these reports in the preparation of their various databases.

Redundancy should be built into any good safety system. I argue that Metra, the Chicago-area commuter rail service, should operate their trains with two people in the locomotive or control cab cars. This argument is supported in various ways: Metra's high number of incidents, the request made and disapproved by then Metra Director of Safety Dennis Mogan to Metra's higher management many years ago (see "Lunch with Dennis Mogan"), and testimony in various chapters by experienced locomotive engineers who had previously worked at freight lines where there is a two-person operating crew with both an engineer and a conductor operating the train.

In the "Tragedy on the Tracks" school-bus-versus-train chapter, I write about the dangers of engineer fatigue. Having one person work long split shift days is a poor way to manage risk. Having two people simultaneously man trains provides an additional layer of safety.

Railroad grade crossings can be made safer by the addition of supplemental safety measures, such as median strips and four-quadrant gates. The chapters that address the Rose Tani, Tristian Hicks Williams, and Lauren Wilson collisions support this claim. These collisions probably would not have occurred if such measures had been in place. We know people go around railroad gates for any number of reasons—one being that it is easy to do—and the results are often tragic.

The work safety record of a locomotive engineer should not be flawed by repeated rule violations. Dennis Mogan, in the chapter "Lunch with Dennis Mogan" indicated that Metra would not have hired the locomotive engineer operating the Metra commuter train (see chapter "Derailment at Milepost 4.7 #2) had they received a complete work record from the prior employer. Mr. Mogan wants complete disclosure to be a requirement when an engineer leaves one railroad company to work at another. The locomotive engineer involved in the Amtrak-versus-truck collision in Bourbonnais had been terminated twice for safety infractions (see "The City of New Orleans"), and yet was rehired. Not the best way to manage risk.

The final two chapters of the book relate to trespasser incidents. This is one area where railroad safety advocates believe much can be done to improve safety, but there seems to be little effort.

In the chapter that covers the Fox River Grove train collision with a school bus, I wrote the following comment: "**We soon found out how important seconds and inches were when it came to life or death**." Steve Laffey, in his editing comments, indicated that this was one of the most important statements made and asked me to repeat it in the introduction. As you read on, you will realize why.

The DuPage Railroad
Safety Council

. . .

CHICAGO IS THE HUB OF railroading in this country, and it is the only city in the United States with six Class 1 freight railroads traveling through it. Class 1 carriers are the big rail lines, such as the Burlington Northern Santa Fe, Union Pacific, and CSX. About six hundred freight trains pass through Chicago and its suburbs daily.

The Northeast Illinois Regional Commuter Railroad Corporation, known as Metra, is the region's commuter rail carrier. Metra runs about seven hundred trains on eleven separate rail lines each weekday. Some of these eleven lines are owned and operated by Metra, and others are operated under purchase-of-service agreements by the Union Pacific and the Burlington Northern Santa Fe railroads. In this book, I will refer to specific accidents involving Metra trains as Metra/NIRC for Metra owned lines, Metra/UP, and Metra/BNSF for Metra purchase-of-service lines. Metra's eleven rail lines cover about thirty-seven hundred square miles and serve more than one hundred communities at 240 rail stations throughout Chicago's Cook County and its collar counties.

Amtrak, the nation's passenger rail system, also has about one hundred movements into and out of Chicago daily.

As of August 1, 2013, there were 2,283 grade crossings in Chicago's Cook County, and in the collar counties of DuPage, Kane, Lake, McHenry, Will, Kenosha, and Kendall. Trains, trains, and more trains pass through hundreds of street-level crossings trafficked by thousands of vehicles and people on a continual basis. Most of Metra's train movements occur during the busy rush hour periods of the day.

Many of the trains going to and from Chicago, especially along the Metra/BNSF and Metra/UP West lines, travel through DuPage County. DuPage County is a congested suburban area, and, according to the 2012 census, has a population of 927,987.

In this book, I make frequent use of the words *accident, collision*, and *incident*. One railroad safety expert suggested not using the word *accident*, which implies it was an unavoidable event and does not bring contributing factors into play. However, *accident* seems to be the word of choice that is used by newspapers and official documents such as NTSB accident reports. When I use any of the three words—*accident, collision* or *incident*—there are contributing factors; there always are. Eliminating or changing any one of the negative contributing factors would reduce the probability of a similar event occurring.

Shortly after the collision that killed Lauren Wilson on March 2, 1994, DuPage County Board President Aldo Botti called for a railroad safety summit. The Chicago area had been plagued with far too many rail crossing accidents. In the four years since January 1, 1990, Metra, when combining all its lines, had been involved in 185 accidents with forty-eight killed and fifty-seven injured.

The railroad safety summit led to the formation of the DuPage Railroad Safety Council (DRSC) in April 1994. The DRSC has continued to meet almost every month since then. The early meeting attendance—I was there when the DRSC was formed—was divided almost equally between those that had a strong knowledge of railroading and those of us who knew very little about railroading (see appendix).

Many people have attended the meetings over the years, volunteering their time and efforts to improve rail safety. A typical DRSC meeting would attract between fifteen and twenty-five people with the mix continually changing. Some members would attend almost every meeting, while others would attend infrequently. Some were railroad people, and others were not. Several had friends or family members who had been injured or killed in train accidents. Dr. Lanny Wilson, the DRSC's only chairman, has the unique ability to keep such a diverse group of people on point and working together in a considerate and thoughtful manner, with the singular goal of improving railroad safety.

Over the many years I attended meetings, the one common thread that ran throughout them was how well we all seemed to work together. Early on, I learned that each of the railroads operating in Chicago and its suburbs has a unique set of operating rules, despite their operating through suburban communities a very short distance from one another.

I also learned, as a result of my involvement with the DRSC and in my investigation of train accidents, that there usually are several predictable contributing factors that come together at one horrific moment in time to create a train accident. We often know what these factors are, yet they are repeated time and time again. We know how to eliminate many of these factors. We also know that by just eliminating any one of these contributing factors we will make great strides in decreasing the probability of an accident occurring or in reducing the severity of an accident that may occur.

At one of our first DRSC 1994 meetings, Wayne Solomon, a locomotive engineer for the former Chicago and North Western Railroad, told me his train was involved in five to seven near hits a day. Wayne also said he served on his railroad's safety committee, which had recommended only one passenger train at a time be allowed in a station that had a street or pedestrian at grade cross-ing. Other trains, whether passenger or freight, must hold out of the station, or only pass through the station when certain very spe-cific safety criteria are met. The recommendation eventually led to special instruction 6.30, meant to eliminate pedestrian versus train accidents. The railroad industry as a whole is governed by a set of general operating rules. When a specific railroad modifies a general operating rule that is used by a group of railroads to suit that rail-road's specific needs the modified rule is called a *special instruction*.

I learned at other meetings that the Metra/NIRC, Union Pacific, CSX, and other rail lines have essentially the same hold out operating rule, while the BNSF Railway, which operates about 160 trains a day on a three-track system through not only my town of Downers Grove but also many other suburban communities, does not require trains to hold out when there is a commuter train either in or exiting the station.

The hold out rule is essential for safety. Many train accidents are not the result of the first train coming down the tracks, but of a sec-ond train that is often ignored. That second train may be traveling in the same direction, but on a different track and hidden by the first train, or it may be traveling in the opposite direction. Too often, the second train is the one involved in the accident.

Someone suggested early on at a DRSC meeting that a recogniz-able second-train warning system would be beneficial in prevent-ing accidents by alerting people that another train is in the area. According to Dennis Mogan, then Metra's safety director, a second-train warning system was already in place on Metra's BNSF com-muter line. The BNSF system works by sounding chimes from the time the first train enters the warning zone until it proceeds through the crossing. It will then be silenced until a second train enters the warning zone, the chimes will sound again even if the lights are still flashing and the gates are still down from the *previous* train. If there are two trains in the warning zone area at the same time, the chimes will continue to sound until both trains have entered the crossing. So if the chimes are still sounding after a train has entered a crossing, then another train is approaching the station.

The BNSF had instituted this second-train warning system at crossings in DuPage and Cook Counties before I was ever involved in railroad safety. Unfortunately, most people do not recognize it as a second-train warning system and pay little, if any, attention to it. My office is near several Downers Grove crossings, and I see firsthand that most people have no idea that a second-train warning system exists along the BNSF. In 1994, the DRSC discussed adding visual and verbal warnings to the system, and Illinois Commerce Commission railroad safety program administrator Bernie Morris indicated state funds were available for the project. Twenty years have passed and the same second train warning system exists on the BNSF Chicagoland system. Today, as before, few people have an understanding of what the chimes mean as it relates to a second train approaching.

With its six grade crossings, Downers Grove in 1994 was one of the most accident-prone railroad cities in Illinois. Almost every year, Illinois is ranked among the top three states in the nation for railroad accidents. Based on the raw numbers of accidents, Texas and California were most often the other two states.

The lack of awareness of the second-train warning system has long been a sore spot with me because second trains have been deadly in my community. Another rail line, the Metra/UP West line, has recently installed a much enhanced second-train warning system in nearby communities. Many Metra/UP West line stations have platforms designed to divert commuters behind warning pedestrian gates at the stations. They also have audio and illuminated visual warnings.

In April 2012 the FRA published "Guidance on Pedestrian Crossing Safety at or Near Passenger Stations."

Installation of station signage and channelizing fencing to guide pedestrians away from the station platform and toward the desired safe crossing point.

*An example of a "Second train coming" display sign used
on a passenger station platform. A verbal announcement
is also delivered on the public address system.*

The DRSC also learned that the freight carriers generally have two people in the locomotive compartment of the train: an engineer and a conductor. Both have the ability to stop the train. Train signals are called out between the two, so the likelihood of missing a track signal is remote. Two people are in a position to not only react to danger, but to alert each other of imminent danger. The second person can read out speed restrictions and special instructions so that the engineer never has to look away from the controls or the windshield. It is a redundancy system similar to that of a pilot and copilot flying a commercial plane.

In any critical safety system, redundancy is an important safeguard. However, Metra commuter trains have only one person, the engineer, in the locomotive compartment operating the train. Metra's single-locomotive engineer system fails to provide the redundancy that is essential for safety. Many times over the years, I have heard from Metra's locomotive engineers how very dangerous they feel it is to operate their trains alone.

There is usually more than one factor contributing to a transportation accident, such as operator fatigue, bad weather, track conditions, inexperience, poor visibility, or equipment problems. Transportation safety experts have long known that human factors or operator errors, often caused by operator fatigue, are contributing factors in as many as one-third of railroad accidents and leading factors in other transportation accidents. (Peña 1995)

Trains are required to sound train horns fifteen to twenty seconds prior to reaching a crossing unless in a quiet zone. Typically, when they reach a whistle post about one-quarter mile from a grade crossing, they will sound their train horns. The horn is meant to provide an additional warning that a train is approaching. According to Federal Railroad Administration (FRA) statistics, as of early 2013, about twenty-nine hundred of the 129,000 public crossings in this country are exempt from mandatory horn-blowing and are called "quiet-zone" crossings. In the seven-county area of Cook and its collar counties (Kenosha, Lake, McHenry, Kane, DuPage, Will), of almost 1,500 grade crossings, over seven hundred are in "quiet zones."

Quiet zones are crossings where whistle blowing is generally discretionary on the part of the locomotive engineer. If the engineer sees the need to blow the train whistle for whatever reason, he or she will do so, and they can do so at any distance from the crossing—or they may not blow the whistle at all.

However, there is a least one exception to the generally excepted quiet zone rule. It is an Illinois rule titled *Other Warnings* that reads; "In addition to warnings by whistle, bell, or horn as required by statute, every train shall give a prolonged or repeated whistling when passing or meeting or about to pass or meet a train in the immediate vicinity of a grade crossing, under such circumstances that the second train will materially obscure the view of the first mentioned train to persons who may be about to use the crossing." (Illinois Administrative Code, Title 92: Transportation: Chapter III: Section 1535.502 n.d.)

It is my opinion that the rule although well intended is subject to interpretation by locomotive engineers and has little impact on improving rail safety. Time and time again, on the BNSF tracks in my community, trains passing stopped or exiting trains in a station either do not sound their horn, or give just a brief horn sounding as the front end of the passing train has almost completely passed the other train.

A review of Illinois railroad accident statistics highlights how dangerous railroad crossings can be. In Chicago and its suburbs, grade-crossing accidents occur on a regular basis.

Region	All Collisions: 1990—2012					
	Collisions	Percent	Killed	Percent	Injured	Percent
Illinois	4,829		805		1,933	
Percentage of Illinois Collisions, Fatalities and Injuries in 7-County Northeastern Region						
Seven-County	1,982	41.0%	330	41.0%	761	39.4%
Percentage of Seven-County Collisions, Fatalities, and Injuries by Type of Train						
Amtrak	96	4.8%	38	11.5%	31	4.1%
Car(s)	9	0.5%	0	0.0%	4	0.5%
Freight	767	38.7%	97	29.4%	271	35.6%
Lite Locos [Light Locomotives]	172	8.7%	10	3.0%	56	7.4%
Metra (NIRC, UP, BNSF)	651	32.8%	178	53.9%	343	45.1%
MOW [Maintenance of Way] Equipment	48	2.4%	1	0.3%	11	1.4%
Yard/Switch	239	12.1%	4	1.2%	45	5.9%

Source: Illinois Commerce Commission

At each monthly DRSC meeting, the various committees would report on what they accomplished between meetings and what actions they thought should take place. Much was accomplished. The DRSC spearheaded changes to increase penalties throughout Illinois for pedestrians and drivers who violated activated railroad warning gates and signals; provided emotional and meaningful railroad safety videos to high school driver education classes throughout Illinois; held day-long biannual meetings inviting first responders, government officials, railroad officials, and the press to discuss railroad safety issues; and testified before government committees on railroad safety issues.

Communities were encouraged to strongly enforce crossing violation laws, and many did. Downers Grove's Police Chief George Graves began posting his officers at grade crossings on a fairly regular basis. Both drivers and pedestrians were ticketed for violations. At one time in Downers Grove, there was a pedestrian herd mentality at grade crossings. When a passenger train unloaded its passengers and pulled out of the station, commuters, while the gates were still down, would immediately cross the tracks. With enforcement, these crossing violations were eventually dramatically reduced. The rush-hour herd mentally became a thing of the past.

Other suburban communities also started to put strong emphasis on enforcing crossing violation laws. Officer Jim Kveton of the Elmhurst Police Department was especially creative with positive enforcement, acknowledging pedestrians who obeyed crossing warning signals with gift certificates to local stores.

Illinois fines for violating crossing gate laws were dramatically increased to $500 for both drivers and pedestrians. That got a lot of press and surely helped educate many.

The Illinois General Assembly authorized a pilot program to evaluate the effectiveness of video enforcement, and Naperville installed it at the River Road (DOT/AAR 079549D) grade crossing. At a monthly DRSC meeting, Naperville Police Officer Jim Bedell showed videos of violations by automobiles at that crossing and explained that violations had dropped once drivers became aware that photo enforcement was in place and tickets were being issued. Eighteen months after the video enforcement began at the River Road crossing, violations dropped to forty-one a month from a baseline violation rate of 315 per month. That 87 percent decrease in violations greatly reduced the probability of a train accident at the River Road crossing.

DRSC Chairman Lanny Wilson and his son publicized the rail safety effort in a television interview on a local TV station. With the help of James Churchill from the State Board of Education, the video, "Railroad Safety," was sent to driver education programs at eight hundred high schools throughout Illinois. The response from driver education teachers was positive.

As one of the persons distributing this video, I gave one to the driver education teacher who operated a driving school located next to my accounting office. After showing the video to his students, he commented that many in his class were either crying or teary-eyed. He learned that among his driver education students were classmates and friends of Lauren Wilson. Tragic accidents impact so many in a community.

As the DRSC continued its work, a three-person subcommittee was formed to investigate local train accidents. I was the subcommittee's chairman and its only active member. Knowledge is power, and it didn't take long for me to learn about railroad safety issues. I was learning from the experts, people like Wayne Solomon from the UP, Dennis Mogan from Metra, Tom Zapler from the UP, and many others. They had much to say, and, to their credit, they seemed to hold little back. When I asked a question, I knew I was going to get the answer.

The more I learned, the more passionate I became about the need to improve safety and better manage risk.

There was a period of time—about five years—that I did not attend DRSC meetings. When I started to attend meetings again there were many new members whom I had not met before. Soon, I realized that nothing had really changed. I was surrounded by smart people giving their time to improve safety on the tracks. I am still not sure how Chairman Lanny Wilson has kept us on point and working together and in a friendly and uplifting way for over twenty years, but to his credit he has done so.

Accident Investigation

. . .

October 25, 1994, Poplar Street, Elmhurst

THE FIRST TRAIN ACCIDENT I investigated would lead to a change in the way trains operate in the United States. It also illustrates how slowly the railroad industry reacts to fairly well-known ways to operate more safely. The accident occurred within days after the DuPage Railroad Safety Council formed its accident review subcommittee, and I learned of the accident from a radio report. I later learned more details of the incident from a *Chicago Sun-Times* article.

Elmhurst, Illinois, is about ten miles from where I live. On the morning of October 25, 1994, sixty-eight-year-old Charlene Bentz left a note for her husband that she had gone out for a brisk walk. It was just after six o'clock in the morning when, according to witnesses, she walked around downed gates and crossed the tracks at the Poplar Street grade crossing (DOT/AAR 174020S) and walked in front of an eastbound Metra/UP West line commuter train operating on the Union Pacific rail line. She was killed. Deputy Police Chief Ralph O'Connell indicated it was the seventh fatality in the last five years at an Elmhurst rail crossing. (O'Connor, Elmhurst Woman Dies Trying to Beat Train 1994)

It was October 26, at 5:50 a.m., the morning after when I first went to the accident location. I had heard that professional investigators typically go back to the scene of the accident the next day, at the same time as the accident had occurred, when conditions are similar. They try to get a better understanding of what took place, to find witnesses to the accident, and to determine what contributing factors may have led to the accident. To my surprise, I was the only person at the scene. I typed the following notes after visiting the accident scene.

Re: Elmhurst Accident Tuesday, October 25, 1994, 6:03 a.m.

On Wednesday, October 26, 1994, I visited the accident scene. I arrived at the Poplar Street crossing at 5:50 a.m. and stayed at the location for twenty minutes.

It was still dark out. The crossing, like several other crossings in Elmhurst, is not well-lit.

At the crossing, there is sidewalk only on the west. There are pedestrian gates at both [the] northwest and southwest sides. The one on the southwest did not have lights or bells, just the down arm. However, there seemed to be many warning lights throughout the crossing when considered as a whole.

At around six o'clock in the morning, a train stopped at the Elmhurst station, which [is] approximately a half mile west of the Poplar Street crossing. The train was at the station for maybe three minutes. The gates were up, and no warning devices were activated [at the Poplar Street crossing] when the train was in the [Elmhurst] station. I was looking at the sweep second hand on my watch. It took approximately fifteen seconds after the bells went off and the gates went down for the train to reach the Poplar Street crossing. It was hard for me to see when the train left the station. It was traveling quite fast when it passed me, maybe thirty-five to forty miles per hour.

Some suggestions that might improve safety:

1) More light at the crossing. This would give the engineer a better view of the whole crossing.
2) Slow the eastbound trains coming out of the station at dark. There are three crossings, including Poplar Street, within about a mile of the station.
3) Maybe have the engineer flash his headlight when the train starts moving out of the station when it is dark.

I did not investigate the accident; I only went to the location a day after the accident. My observations are of the location some twenty-four hours after the accident.

Poplar Street crossing, Elmhurst

As I sensed immediately, the sooner one is able to recognize that a train is approaching—or a locomotive engineer is able to recognize a possible danger ahead—the less likelihood there is of a accident occurring.

What I found extremely troubling that morning was that the train was almost invisible to the eye as it sat in the station just about half a mile away. It wasn't due to the fact that the station wasn't illuminated that dark morning; there were many lit street and station lights. In addition to the station lights, there was also one fixed twin headlight set high and centered on the lead car of the train. The problem was that everything blended together; giving the illusion that there was no train in the station. There was nothing about the train's lighting pattern that made it uniquely recognizable as a train.

A locomotive pushes or pulls Metra trains: it pushes the train on the return trip, and pulls the train when leaving Chicago. Such was the case here. The locomotive engineer who operated the train did so from a front section of the lead car known as the control cab car. This lead control cab car also serves as a passenger car. There was just a single set of fixed twin headlights centered high on this cab car.

Metra cab car without triangular lighting

This is what I was soon to learn from some fairly basic observations: In 1994, Metra commuter line locomotives had very uniquely recognizable and enhanced triangular lighting systems. The locomotives were equipped with low-lying ditch lights on each side of the front end and a fixed and oscillating headlight set higher up in the middle. These lights formed a very recognizable triangular pattern on the front of the train. These lights were visible twenty-four hours a day when the locomotive was pulling the train from Chicago. An approaching Metra locomotive with the distinctive triangular lighting system in place was quickly recognized as an approaching train.

Triangular lighting

Many of Metra's lines operated with control cab cars having only the high-set fixed twin headlight, and not the triangular lighting pattern, which made the approaching train difficult to recognize.

In 1994, one busy Metra commuter rail line, the Metra/BN (now BNSF), had both the locomotives and the control cab cars operating with the enhanced triangular lighting pattern.

Metra cab car with triangular lighting

In 1995, I began reviewing Metra fatal accidents. Commuter trains operating with the enhanced triangular lighting pattern were far safer than trains operating without the enhanced triangular lighting. It was obvious that enhanced triangular lighting was making a difference.

Ditch lights also were mounted on almost all the freight train locomotives that I observed, but they were not being used. Freight train locomotives had the single headlight system with that high fixed light constantly on, while their ditch lights—which, if used, would have formed the unique triangular pattern—were turned off.

Freight trains were not required to have their ditch lights lit. I observed that in late 1996, the train locomotives on two of our country's biggest Class I freight lines, the BN (now BNSF) and UP lines, did not typically operate with these low-set ditch lights on, either during the day or at night.

On October 25, 1995 in Fox River Grove, Illinois, a collision between a Metra/UP Northwest line train and a school bus killed seven students and injured twenty-nine students. The nation was in shock. This collision involved a lead Metra/UP control cab car without enhanced triangular lighting. There will be much more about this collision in later chapters. If the school bus driver or the bus passengers would have recognized that a train was approaching, the collision may either have been avoided, or, if it did occur, there may very well have been fewer deaths and injuries.

After the 1994 Poplar Street accident, I learned much about enhanced lighting, the triangular light pattern, and how much safer railroading would be if approaching trains were more recognizable. I strongly advocated the use of the lights, both verbally and in writing—during DRSC meetings and in letters to the editor printed in newspapers, to the National Transportation Safety Board, to the administrator of the Federal Railroad Administration (FRA), President Clinton and to whoever else might listen. Most people turned a deaf ear to what I was saying. After the horrific Fox River Grove collision, a government hearing that focused on mandatory train horn blowing was held on March 16, 1996. FRA Administrator Jolene Molitoris and a number of politically powerful Illinois congressmen, including Henry Hyde, Harris Fawell, and John E. Porter, attended to hear witness testimony. I testified that trains with the enhanced triangular lighting pattern were simply much safer than those without it. I indicated that federal regulations only "encouraged" their usage, but would *not require* the enhanced triangular lighting *until December 31, 1997.* I asked that someone with authority ask the railroads to just flip the switch now and turn on these ditch lights on freight train locomotives.

Prior to the hearing, I had expressed my feelings about the safety value of enhanced lighting to President Clinton and had received a detailed and friendly response from FRA Administrator Jolene Molitoris. However, at the hearing, she seemed visibly upset when I asked her in my testimony if the FRA could tell the railroads to simply turn on the ditch lights that were already on their locomotives.

In fact, the Amtrak Authorization and Development Act of October 27, 1992 specified that "not later than December 31, 1992, the secretary shall issue interim regulations identifying ditch lights, crossing lights, strobe lights, and oscillating lights as interim conspicuity measures, and authorizing and *encouraging* installation and use of such measures." In February 1993, the proposed interim final rule "interim locomotive conspicuity measures—auxiliary external lights" conspicuity rule 49 CFR, Part 229.125 stated in part that "it is the federal policy to *encourage* the installation and use of an auxiliary external light arrangement specified in the section on each locomotive" (emphasis added). The document goes on to say that the lights are not required, and that nonuse will not render the locomotive in noncompliance.

In early 1997, I had a telephone conversation with Gordon Davids of the FRA. He indicated that ditch lights had begun being used on locomotives in Canada ten to fifteen years earlier, and that Canadian trains had far fewer accidents when the ditch lights were on.

In January 1996, I received a copy of an FRA document, "Locomotive Visibility: Minimum Standards for Auxiliary Lights" (July 1995), from George Cochran, an NTSB railroad accident investigator, when I attended an NTSB hearing on the Fox River Grove collision. The report estimated that with more conspicuous and enhanced locomotive lighting there would be sixty-three hundred fewer train accidents, with fifteen hundred fewer fatalities, and three thousand fewer accidents over the next twenty years.

The 1992 Amtrak Authorization and Development act required that final regulations requiring enhanced locomotive conspicuity be issued no later than June 30, 1995. The final regulation required that all train locomotives, with some minor exceptions, have the enhanced triangular lighting installed and turned on twenty-four hours a day no later than December 31, 1997. It seemed that many major freight carriers were waiting until that last possible moment to turn on the lights that had already been installed on their trains.

Metra, on some of its lines, began installing ditch lights on their control cab cars in 1992 and would be in full compliance by the mandated requirement date of December 31, 1997, according to a March 12, 1997 letter I received from NTSB Chairman Jim Hall. But what is so disturbing is that the railroads—Metra included—either knew or should have known many years prior to December 31, 1997 what a huge improvement in safety these enhanced lighting systems would make. I knew it. So, the question is why were they not turned on?

In late 1996, I sent information about enhanced lighting to the chief executives of all the major Class 1 freight rail carriers and asked them to make Christmas brighter and safer for everyone by turning on their locomotive safety ditch light systems all hours of the day. Included in my mailing was a published editorial piece I had written on the subject and references to the FRA document about locomotive visibility. Within a couple of weeks after sending my letter to CEOs, these ditch lights started going on and the triangular lights of freight train locomotives were lit twenty-four hours a day. Accidents immediately started to decline.

By looking out of my office window, which at the time had a clear view of the BNSF tracks, I knew immediately when the ditch lights started going on. I remember sending a short note to Dr. Lanny Wilson of the DRSC telling him the ditch lights were going on and that perhaps his daughter, Lauren, is the angel who had brought it about. She truly is.

A dozen or so years later, I attended a DuPage Railroad Safety Council meeting where a rail crossing safety expert, but not a member of the DRSC, graphically demonstrated how significantly railroad accidents had declined since 1996. When I asked what he thought the reason was, he attributed that to the ditch-light effect. When ditch lights went on, accidents went down.

Railroad accidents have continued to steadily decrease on an annual basis, according to statistics compiled by the Federal Railroad Administration.

Year	Highway/rail collisions	Deaths
1996	4,257	488
2001	3,237	421
2006	3,066	369
2009	1,925	247

The following graph reflects the decrease in both collisions and deaths at railroad grade crossings just in Illinois.

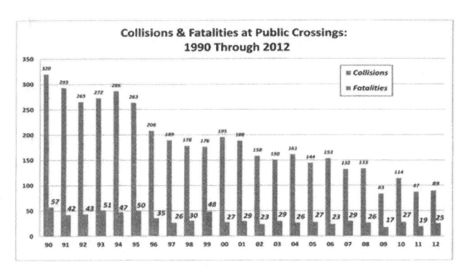

Source: Illinois Commerce Commission

It took the flip of a switch—something that could have taken place many years before 1996. When the ditch lights were finally turned on and a triangular lighting pattern formed, people began to more readily recognize approaching trains. The sooner they recognized a train approaching, the more time they had to react.

One predictable contributing factor in rail safety—the nonrecognition of an approaching train—became less frequent, and with that, railroad collisions decreased dramatically.

The Volpe Center is a well-known and highly respected research and innovative technology center that is part of the US Department of Transportation. As early as the 1970s, "the Volpe Center conducted several studies on improving train conspicuity through use of locomotive alerting lights, such as oscillating headlights, rotating beacons, crossing lights, ditch lights, ground lights, and roof mounted strobe lights. Field evaluations showed that two strobe lights used in a triangular configuration with a standard highlight was the most effective system... FRA published rulemaking initiatives on [the] use of auxiliary external alerting light systems in 1978, 1979, and 1982. Public comments, however, raised questions on alerting light effectiveness, cost, and reliability, and the initiatives were discontinued...The results of controlled field tests indicated that the triangular lighting pattern with each type of auxiliary lights (crossing, ditch, and strobe) increased detectability of the locomotive compared to the use of the standard headlights alone. Each system provided a distinctive uniform light pattern that motorists could recognize as signifying a locomotive." (Federal Railroad Administration 2007)

In December 2011, the FRA in a published paper indicated that from 1994 to 2007 there was a 44.7 percent decline in highway-rail grade crossing collisions. In the paper locomotive conspicuity was named as one of the most significant factors that led to this dramatic reduction. (Federal Railroad Administration 2011)

Deadly Second Train

. . .

FAIRVIEW AVENUE, DOWNERS GROVE

SINCE ITS INCEPTION, THE DuPAGE Railroad Safety Council was fortunate to have many railroad professionals in attendance. Almost immediately, we discussed the high percentage of Chicago-area rail accidents that were caused by a second train. One railroad safety expert in the group estimated that as many as one-third of the accidents were the result of second trains—not the train the accident casualty is focused on: the train stopped at the station, the one that had just discharged passengers and was in the process of exiting the station, or the train that had just passed them at the crossing. The second train was the one involved in the accident—the train that may have been out of sight, and definitely out of mind. Drivers, commuters, and pedestrians often make tragic judgment errors, believing the crossing to be safe when, in fact, it is very unsafe.

With gates down, warning lights flashing, and warning chimes sounding, drivers and pedestrians often violate these deterrents and attempt to cross the tracks. That is when the unseen second train passes through the station, or arrives from the opposite direction, or overtakes a slower approaching train or a train stopped on the tracks and becomes involved in a accident. If people were made more aware of the second train, the number of these accidents would decline. Accidents would be prevented, and lives would be saved.

Second-train accidents can and do occur anywhere along the tracks. In the preface, I recounted the train accident that started me thinking about railroad safety. On September 29, 1989, I was involved in an auto accident and, as I was being rushed by ambulance to Hinsdale Hospital, I could hear over the ambulance radio paramedics at a different accident scene. Young Jonathan Goers had just been struck by a train. I could hear the urgency in their voices as they communicated with doctors while treating eleven-year-old Jonathan.

Many years later, I learned that one train had just passed when Jonathan attempted to cross the tracks. The train that was involved in the accident was that second train. The Monroe Street crossing in Hinsdale is not adjacent to a commuter station. It is a relatively quiet crossing in a residential area.

The tragic death of ninety-year-old Rose Tani on December 19, 2007, would normally not have been a highly publicized collision, except that her son, astronaut Daniel Tani, was in space circling earth when it occurred. Mrs. Tani drove around a crossing gate at the Elizabeth Street (DOT/AAR 174944W) crossing in Lombard, and her car was struck by a train. According to witnesses, a train had just passed, the gates went up briefly allowing a couple of cars to cross, and then descended again. Rose Tani drove around a stopped school bus and the downed gate and was struck by a second train. Like Hinsdale's Monroe Street crossing, the Elizabeth Street crossing is located in a relatively quiet residential neighborhood.

However, far too many second-train accidents do take place at crossings near busy commuter stations. Often there are many vehicles, commuters, and pedestrians waiting for arriving, stopped, or exiting trains. There are many distractions such as cell phones, conversations between passengers, and headphones. Often people in a rush pay little attention to their immediate surroundings.

In the 1990s, as today, Chicago and its suburbs experienced far too many train accidents, as attested to by several newspaper articles from the period:

* "11 Killed in Last 3 Weeks on Metra Tracks," including at least two accidents involving second trains. (O'Connor and Golab, 11 Killed in Last 3 Weeks on Metra Tracks 1994)
* "In the last four years in Illinois, nearly 200 people have died where roads meet train tracks—nearly half of them in the Chicago area." (Kerrill, Deadly Crossings Plague State 1995)
* "Accidents at train crossings happen so frequently that Chicago and 143 suburbs—nearly two thirds of the communities in the metropolitan area—have experienced more than 800 crashes in the last seven years, a Sun-Times analysis shows." (Kerrill, Area's Train Crossings: 800 Crashes In 7 Years 1995)

In all, there were 284 train accidents and forty-six fatalities in Illinois during 1994, according to the Illinois Commerce Commission.

It is now 2015, and train accidents are still commonplace in Chicago and its suburbs, and Illinois is routinely ranked among the three states with the highest number of train accidents and fatalities.

"Suburbs fail to mirror state's drop in train collisions," according to a headline in the Daily Herald. "At least three people a month will die when they are hit by a train in the Chicago region next year, according to statistical forecasts," wrote reporter Marni Pyke. (Pyke, In Harm's Way 2012)

At one of our first DRSC meetings, Wayne Solomon, a locomotive engineer with the former Chicago and North Western Railway (C&NW), explained that different rail lines operating in the Chicago suburbs have significantly different operating rules. Chicago, the major railroad operating hub in the United States, has several major rail lines that the Metra commuter line shares with freight lines. In 1994, there were the C&NW (merged with the UP in April 1995), the Burlington Northern, Norfolk and Southern, and others. Metra operated each of its commuter lines under a unique set of rules.

Retired engineer Steve Frankowiak commented that you can fly an airliner anywhere in the world using one set of rules, but you can't run a train across Chicago without at least four different sets of rules, signals, or safety systems.

The C&NW did not allow trains to enter a station if a commuter train was either in the station or in the process of exiting a station, Mr. Solomon said. The approaching train had to hold out until the train in the station had moved on and there was no longer a danger with that second train passing through the station. Mr. Solomon had been on the C&NW safety committee that recommended the rule to management. It was just too dangerous for trains to pass through a station when another train was stopped or exiting it, he explained. Without this rule, there had been too many second train accidents.

When I asked him how the C&NW was able to maintain an orderly flow of train traffic with the hold out rule, Mr. Solomon stressed the importance of train scheduling.

At one of our early DRSC meetings, Bernard Morris, railroad safety program administrator for the Illinois Commerce Commission, explained that the pedestrian warning gate system was never designed or instituted to protect or warn commuters getting off the train. The warning system was designed for pedestrians and cars approaching the crossing. Detraining commuters walk on the station platform directly parallel with the train. The pedestrian warning gates are set too far back from the crossing, at about 12 feet from the track, to protect them.

When the train leaves the station, commuters often cross regardless of the dangers that may still lurk on the tracks. C. E. Doggett, division superintendent for the Chicago division of the Burlington Northern in a letter to me stated, "I disagree with Mr. Morris that the pedestrian warning system was never designed or put in place to warn commuters. Commuters <u>are pedestrians</u> and, as such, should never walk along the train and cross the tracks. They should cross at the designated pedestrian crossing, obeying pedestrian warning signals and gates. As information, the warning bells are there to provide and additional audible warning for those who insist on ignoring pedestrian gates. Pedestrian crosswalks and warning devices are designated for all pedestrians, but only effective if pedestrians allow them to work for them." (Doggett 1994)

Tom Zapler of the Union Pacific, and a member of the DRSC, gave me a copy of "Special Instruction L Rule 6.30" that went into very specific detail on when an approaching train could enter a station if a commuter train was stopped or exiting. This special instruction stated that trains must stop before entering an occupied commuter station and could only enter under certain safe conditions. The Union Pacific continued to operate the former C&NW line with this rule in place after it acquired the railroad in 1995.

In 1994, Ken Lanman, the regional manager for highway-rail crossing safety for the Federal Railroad Administration's Chicago suburban region, and a member of the DRSC, gave me detailed track maps of rail lines within the Chicago suburban rail system. These track maps showed where track crossovers, signal towers, and stations were located. They also indicated other important track information.

Ten of Metra's eleven rail lines almost eliminated one contributing factor in second-train accidents at or near commuter stations. Stringent operating rules restrict the movement of trains through a commuter station that is occupied by a commuter train or where a commuter train is in the process of exiting the station.

At the August 27, 1994, meeting of the DRSC, Dennis Mogan, then Metra's director of safety and rules, reported that the Burlington Northern's grade crossing appliances through the Hinsdale-Downers Grove area are as sophisticated as any in the industry. He went on to explain that the system isn't the type of warning most people know about, and in fact means nothing to most commuters. If there is a train within a certain distance from the crossing on any of the three tracks, lights go on, the gates come down, and there are warning chimes sounding. When a commuter train stops at the station or enters the crossing, the gates remain down, but the warning chimes stop and remain silent until a second train approaches.

Then, even with the gates in a down position, the chimes that had been silenced will reactivate and sound again when a second approaching train triggers the warning. These types of crossings would be an ideal application to consider for both lit and verbal warnings that would alert those at the crossing of the approaching of a second train. Bernie Morris of the Illinois Commerce Commission indicated at the time that there was money available to fund such a project. In fact, his staff considered a pilot project for this type of enhancement. Remember, this is back in the mid-1990s.

In September 1994, several suburban newspapers published articles about the formation of the DuPage Railroad Safety Council and its subcommittee for the investigation of train accidents and mentioned my name. Many on the DRSC were not railroad people and we had much to learn. We instinctively thought something could be learned by investigating railroad accidents.

For me, investigating railroad accidents was not only something new, but was something I was interested in doing. Looking back, my lack of knowledge caused me to ask many questions and spend countless hours reviewing accident details, visiting nearby accident sites, and talking and corresponding with railroad people and safety experts. Almost without exception, everyone was helpful and willing to share their knowledge or observations with me. In fact, I sometimes felt they hoped their shared insights would ultimately improve rail safety. I believe they have.

Within several weeks after the articles about the DRSC's accident investigation subcommittee appeared, I received a call from someone who wanted to discuss a train-pedestrian incident that had occurred in my community of Downers Grove, at a crossing less than a mile from my accounting office.

At the meeting, he indicated that he had worked for a railroad at one point in his career, but now was working as an accident investigator for an attorney. Several years earlier, at Fairview Avenue in Downers Grove, a woman was struck and killed by an express high-speed Metra commuter train.

Pedestrian Incidents

. . .

FAIRVIEW AVENUE, DOWNERS GROVE
AUGUST 26, 1991, AND JUNE 11, 1993

THE METRA/BNSF LINE IS JUST one of eleven Metra rail lines in Chicago and its suburbs. Metra's BNSF line runs between Chicago's Union Station and Aurora, Illinois. The BNSF owns the equipment and hires the employees and, in turn, charges Metra for these contracted costs. The distance between the two cities is about thirty-eight miles and amounts to just a small fraction of the total track miles in Metra's commuter train system, which services about thirty-seven hundred square miles. Although short in distance, it is an extremely busy three-track system, which handles about 160 trains on an average weekday and is one of the busiest in the United States.

Ten of Metra's eleven rail lines have isolated and almost eliminated one type of accident by implementing rules that restrict the movement of trains through a commuter station when the station is occupied by a commuter train or when a commuter train is in the process of exiting the station. Metra/BNSF has not.

One of Downers Grove's six crossings, Fairview Avenue, DOT-AAR 079532A, was considered one of the more accident-prone and deadlier crossings among Illinois's more than ten thousand public grade crossings. An accident investigator who had seen the newspaper article about the DuPage Railroad Safety Council's accident investigation subcommittee visited my office. He had been hired by an attorney representing the estate of the late Mary Wojtyla. Ms. Wojtyla had been struck and killed by a Metra/BNSF train. He told me a little about the accident and gave me a video of it taken by a train buff.

Fairview Avenue, Downers Grove, IL, Metra/BNSF line, August 26, 1991.

It was shot at Fairview Avenue at 5:52 p.m. on August 26, 1991. The stopped westbound Metra/BNSF commuter train number 1231 had just offloaded passengers about fifty feet east of Fairview Avenue. Many commuters detrained and walked west along the platform and crossed the tracks, walking from the north platform to the south platform, where there is a large commuter parking lot. The warning gates were lowered and the warning bells were silenced, but then sounded again. Commuters continued crossing from north to south in front of the stopped train, both when the chimes were silenced and when they again sounded. The warning gates remained down the whole time, but were set so far back on the sidewalk that they were not an effective warning barrier to the commuters walking westward along the platform who wanted to cross the tracks. (R.R. 1991) (Incident 1991)

The westbound Metra/BNSF commuter train stopped east of Fairview Avenue and did not block and protect the crossing. A high-standing signal bridge located just feet west of Fairview would have made it difficult for a locomotive engineer of a westbound commuter train to see the signal aspects if the locomotive was pulled too close. The aerial photo shows clearly how close the signal bridge was to Fairview Avenue.

Aerial view, Fairview Avenue crossing, Downers Grove, Illinois.

Commuters were not channeled behind the warning gates. As commuters continued to cross the tracks, a pair of pedestrians, who had been walking along the sidewalk, went around the gates. They followed the herd mentality of the commuters crossing in front of them, which often occurs at crossings. A second westbound Metra/BNSF express train, number 1245, traveling at about sixty mph down middle track number two of the three-track system, struck and killed a pedestrian, forty-one-year-old Mary Wojtyla. The male pedestrian had stepped back and missed being struck by just inches. As the second train approached, the chimes sounded again, but that didn't deter the many other commuters who had crossed just seconds before the accident. A video camera operated by a train buff captured Mary Wojtyla being struck.

This was an accident waiting to happen—and it would happen again. Just two years later, under an almost identical set of circumstances, on June 11, 1993, sixty-seven-year-old Marie Niedziela walked in front of a stopped Metra/BNSF train at the same Fairview crossing and was struck by a second train. (Downers Grove Police Dept. Incident No. 93-8038 1993)

It's important to note that Marie Niedziela was legally blind. Vision handicaps and poor visibility can be contributing factors in rail accidents. Several of the other accidents reviewed in this book involve poor vision or visibility as a contributing factor. (Drake 1993) (Sudak 1993)

The primary contributing factor was, as before, an express Metra commuter train passing a stopped Metra commuter train at a congested commuter station crossing. Another contributing factor was that the stopped train did not block and protect the crossing.

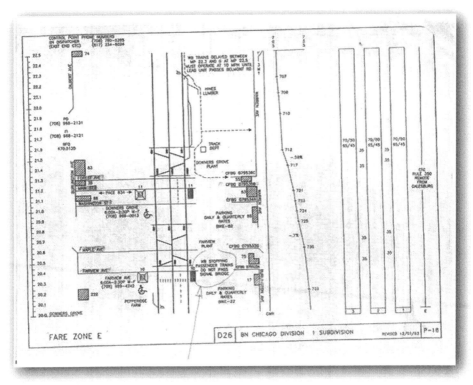

Track Map Fairview Avenue, Downers Grove, IL

Based on the Metra/BNSF schedule that was effective at the time of the accidents, Metra/BNSF train number 1231 was to leave the Fairview Station at 5:48 p.m. to continue west to the Main Street Station in Downers Grove. However, express Metra/BNSF train number 1245, the train involved in the accident, was scheduled to cross in front of Metra/BNSF train number 1231 at a crossover about sixteen hundred feet west of Fairview Avenue and then, using the same northern-most track, stop at the Main Street Station slightly less than a mile away. Train 1245 was scheduled to depart the Main Street station at 5:49 p.m., just two minutes before train number 1231—which followed Metra/BNSF express train number

1245 on the same track into the Main Street station—was scheduled to depart the same station at 5:51 p.m.

Metra/BNSF train number 1231 had to wait at Fairview Station until passed by Metra/BNSF express train number 1245 traveling at about sixty-five mph. When Metra train number 1231 stopped at Fairview station, it wasn't blocking or protecting the crossing during peak evening rush hour. It was effectively out of service until it was passed by Metra/BNSF train number 1245, the express train.

The local train number 1231 was stopped in the station for an unusually long time and was not protecting the crossing, allowing commuters to detrain and then giving both impatient commuters and pedestrians the misguided impression that *it* was the stopped train that had activated the lowered gates. Commuters and pedestrians believed it was OK to walk in front of this train. The sounding of warning chimes when the second train approached had no effect on those who continued to cross—and there were many.

After visiting the accident scene and recalling what engineer Wayne Solomon told me about the importance of scheduling trains, I reviewed the Metra schedule. Metra/BNSF trains numbered 1231 and 1245 were running on a schedule that was beyond dangerous—it was deadly. Metra eventually changed the train schedule so that Metra/BNSF train number 1231 did not have to stay in the Fairview Avenue Station until it was passed by Metra/BNSF express train number 1245. Just maybe, my letter to Metra explaining this danger helped bring about this change.

The accidents that killed Mary Wojtyla and Marie Niedziela were both predictable, and both involved some of the same contributing factors. As I write this about twenty years after both accidents, some of the predictable contributing factors that existed then still exist. Trains still pass Metra/BNSF commuter trains that are stopped in or exiting commuter stations. The second-train warning system that existed in 1991 still exists, but there has been little effort to educate the public about how it works. Commuters are still not channeled behind the warning gates.

Stopped rear end of westbound Metra train as commuters wait in front of downed gate, photo taken May 2014 from my car at Washington Street, Main Street Station, Downers Grove, Illinois

Other Deadly
Second-Train Incidents

. . .

IT IS UP TO EACH railroad to establish operating rules. The Union Pacific's special instruction 6.30 establishes an operating practice specifying when and how passenger and freight trains can enter and pass through a station. This special instruction is followed by all Chicago-area Metra commuter rail lines with one single glaring exception: the BNSF. One purpose of special instruction 6.30 is to make sure that passengers who have just detrained can clear the area safely before the approaching train enters. Operating instruction 6.30 instructs the train engineer when and how he can safely enter the station and when he must hold out.

Trains operating along the BNSF operate at different speeds. Freight trains travel up to forty-five mph, commuter express trains at about sixty-nine mph, and Amtrak trains at about seventy-nine mph. They typically do not slow down when passing through a station, and it means little if the station is occupied with a commuter train, or if a commuter train has just off-loaded passengers and is exiting the station. Metra does not operate these trains. The BNSF, under contract for service with Metra, operates the trains.

Metra/BNSF operates almost one hundred commuter trains every weekday, carrying almost sixty-five thousand commuters to about twenty-five commuter stations. During rush hour, and when special events take place, the stations are congested with people, cars, and trains. There is little, if any, reaction time available for anyone who is on the same track as an approaching train. Once a train is close to the station, the locomotive engineer has little time to brake or slow down the train. A train traveling at sixty-nine mph is moving at about one hundred feet per second. In one collision reviewed, it took about a half mile for a Metra/UP commuter train to stop once braking began at about sixty-nine mph. Freight trains, because of their weight, traveling at slower speeds might require even more distance to stop. Trains take long distances to stop. To this day, the BNSF continues to allow trains to freely pass through stations at high speeds when the stations are occupied by commuter trains, or when commuter trains have just exited the station. These stations are often full of commuters and others.

Almost annually, I make an appearance before the Downers Grove Village Council to talk about the second-train danger in Downers Grove. I talk about how much safer it is along the Metra/UP West line and explain how the warning system works. Hopefully, those watching these televised meetings will become more aware of the dangers at the many crossings we have.

Starting in 1994 I have written, spoken to, or e-mailed BNSF officials about the dangers of letting trains speed through congested and occupied stations without adequate safeguards.

In January 1998, after years of trying to improve safety at station crossings along the BNSF but getting nowhere, I distributed the video of a tragic, second-train accident at Downers Grove's Fairview Avenue crossing to newspapers and television station outlets throughout the Chicago area. Some time ago, I saw parts of the video, with the graphic details omitted, on a TV program featuring the ten worst train accidents. It is also on the Internet.

From 1991 through 2011, there have been at least eight second-train accidents and deaths on the BNSF tracks at crossings near commuter stations that were either occupied or where a commuter train had just exited. Many are not well documented in FRA required reports. In April 2001, I had a lengthy phone conversation with Larry Hasvold, the regional administrator at the Federal Railroad Administration's Chicago office, about second trains passing in stations on the BNSF tracks. He had already been alerted to the danger after the FRA had been contacted by locomotive engineers. But because there is no federal rule preventing this, he could not order trains not to pass in occupied stations. He also indicated that the FRA was working with Amtrak and the BNSF regarding this danger. It is now more than fourteen years since my conversation with Larry Hasvold, and nothing has changed. (Hasvold 2001)

In 2010, thanks to Metra Board Chairman Carole Doris, I was allowed to address Metra's Board of Directors where I expressed my concerns about second-train accidents along the BNSF. The Illinois Commerce Commission also has long been aware of the dangers of trains passing other trains. (Meeting 2010)

The people who had the power or influence to change matters or better educate the public regarding a second-train warning system along the Metra/BNSF railroad line simply didn't do it. Those same people had many years to react to a serious problem and better manage a risk that they were well aware of, yet they chose not to.

• • •

At about six-thirty in the evening on Saturday, March 31, 2001, twenty-year-old Laura Young had just stepped off a westbound Metra/

BNSF commuter train at the Belmont station in Downers Grove. She asked where she could make a phone call, and a fellow passenger indicated the station building on the other side of the tracks. Ms. Young walked to the Belmont crossing (DOT/AAR 079537J) and began to cross the tracks as the Metra train pulled away. The gates started to go up and then came down again. A westbound Amtrak train traveling sixty-nine mph—about one hundred feet per second—struck and killed Ms. Young. She had been born with vision correctable at best to 20/40, according to her obituary. An aspiring teacher who was once told that her poor vision would disqualify her from becoming a missionary, Ms. Young had refused to give up and traveled to Mexico to help build housing for the poor the year prior to her death. (Zemaitis 2001) (Department, Incident #01-6223 2001)

• • •

It was a cold thirty-six-degree Saturday afternoon on November 23, 2003, when Patricia McKenna, forty-eight, exited the eastbound Metra/BNSF train stopped at Hinsdale's Bush Hill Station on the BNSF line. Witnesses commented that visibility was poor due to a wintry mix of precipitation. Ms. McKenna walked to the back of the stopped train on the south side of the tracks and started to cross north at Washington Street (DOT/AAR 079523B), which borders the station at its west end. A westbound freight train traveling down the middle track at about forty-five mph struck Ms. McKenna at 3:07 p.m. She was killed. (Rwy 2003) (Boyle 2003)

• • •

Thursday, January 22, 2004 was a normal workday for thirty-four-year-old Scott Eskew. Mr. Eskew was legally blind and commuted on a regular basis between the Berwyn Station on the Metra/BNSF and his job at the Art Institute of Chicago.

Normally, eastbound trains board on the south platform of the station. But on this day, because of freight train interference, the 1:14 p.m. eastbound train was to stop on the northern platform. Any change in a train's normal stopping pattern is always dangerous because of the resulting confusion on the part of commuters, a railroad official told me.

The station agent made an announcement that the eastbound commuter train would be boarding on the northern platform. Mr. Eskew was standing on the northern platform by the sidewalk at Grove Street when a freight train passed through the station only five to fifteen seconds prior to the arrival of the commuter train. Mr. Eskew stepped onto the tracks and was struck and killed by the Metra/BNSF commuter train.

His estate sued the Burlington Northern & Santa Fe Railway and Metra. At the trial, Daniel Melcher, the plaintiffs' transportation safety expert, testified that the warning system with gates and chimes or bells was inadequate and confusing, that there was no channeling of commuters behind the warning gates, and that the Berwyn Station is a dangerous and high-risk train-pedestrian location.

The jury returned a verdict of five million dollars, assigning 85 percent of the liability to the BNSF, 10 percent of the liability to Metra, and just 5 percent contributory negligence to Mr. Eskew. The circuit court entered a judgment of $4,750,000 in favor of the plaintiffs. The BNSF and Metra appealed the verdict to the appellate court and lost. (Eskew v. Burlington Northern & Santa Fe Ry. Co. 2011) (Scott D. Eskew 2004)

. . .

In Riverside at Longcommon Road (DOT/AAR 079498V) on the BNSF line, Patricia Quane, fifty-two, biked around a stopped Metra/BNSF train that was boarding passengers and was struck and killed by an express train passing through the station on Tuesday, August 23, 2005, at about quarter to eight in the morning. (Oak Park bicyclist killed by Metra train 2005) (B. N. Fe 2005)

. . .

At La Grange Road (DOT/AAR 079508Y) in La Grange, on Friday, December 16, 2005, at 5:26 p.m., Sidney Wiles, in his seventies, walked behind a stopped westbound train and was struck and killed by a passing Metra/BNSF train (Metra train kills pedestrian, 70 2005) (B. N. Fe 2005)

. . .

At about seven o'clock in the evening on Wednesday, November 9, 2011, Sherri Jaskoviak, fifty-one, at Main Street (DOT/AAR 079535V), walked in front of a stopped westbound Metra/BNSF train that was unloading passengers at the Main Street station in Downers Grove and was struck and killed by a westbound freight train operating on the middle track. (Department, Downers Grove Police Department Case #01-11-009122 2011) (Lively 2011) (BNSF 2011)

Meanwhile in 2011, the Union Pacific, on their West Line, first started to allow trains to pass through eight occupied stations, but only after the railroad had made significant safety improvements at the station crossings on that line. The safety improvements included reconfiguring the station platforms so commuters had to walk behind the warning gates on their way to and from the trains, adding verbal warnings indicating that a second train was approaching, and adding warning lights that indicated another train was approaching.

A press release announced the improvements at stations on the Metra/UP West line and noted that second trains would now be allowed to pass through the these stations without adhering to the hold out rule. Significant funding for this project came from the Illinois Department of Transportation:

A new pedestrian grade crossing system is being activated at eight stations on the Union Pacific West Line on March 1, 2011. The Another Train Warning System (ATWS) is part of a $132 million project that aims to improve the flow of commuter and freight traffic on the heavily used line, as well as to allow trains to safely operate past a station when a commuter train is stopped there.

Metra and Union Pacific studied station improvement initiatives across the country and the West Line safety infrastructure is incorporating the best practices, creating the most comprehensive safety system of any commuter rail operation in the U.S.

The ATWS uses audible and visual alerts to warn pedestrians at crossings near the stations that a second train—in addition to the one that is stopped at the station—is approaching or present. The system is being activated at the Maywood, Melrose Park, Elmhurst, Villa Park, Glen Ellyn, College Avenue, Winfield and Geneva stations. It remains active until only one train or no train is present. The system enhances other grade crossing protections, including new paths that safely guide pedestrians to a gated crossing, more pedestrian gates and more fencing to discourage pedestrians from crossing at unsafe and unauthorized locations.

Many years ago, I read an excellent article that argued that government safety regulations are often not as strict as they could or should be. Governmental bodies set relatively low minimum mandatory standards. The businesses impacted—railroads, airlines, manufacturers, and so forth—lobby and argue vigorously for less rigid standards. They come up with any number of reasons why tighter standards should not be implemented: they are too costly, are unfunded mandates, are not possible to achieve, would interfere with operations, and wouldn't make much of a difference. The industry lobbyists are often successful in their efforts. Whatever their reasoning, these groups now have a set of regulations in place that are very achievable, but that do not achieve the most desired safety result needed to best manage risk.

To both improve safety beyond existing minimum safety standards and, at the same time, reduce the probability of a collision occurring would create a double-edged sword for businesses. It might be safer to do something in a different way, but to do it in a way that surpasses the minimum regulations could increase the business's liability exposure when a collision does occur. The higher standard, although not required, would reduce the probability of a collision, but if a collision did occur, litigators could argue that either the operating instructions used to achieve this higher standard for safety were not followed properly, or that the safety equipment failed. Plaintiff's attorneys would now have more favorable arguments to help in winning a lawsuit or to reach a more substantial and meaningful settlement. If there is a probability of something occurring, regardless of how well the risk is managed, it will eventually occur. How often an incident occurs depends on how well risk is managed.

The 1991 Fairview Avenue train-pedestrian accident has been viewed by many on TV and the Internet. Various blogs question the circumstances that led to this horrific video. Unfortunately, all the viewers see is a woman walking in front of a stopped train and being struck by an express train traveling at almost seventy mph. They do not see how many people had walked in front of that same stopped train just prior to the accident. They are not aware of just how dangerous this crossing is and why.

The estate of the victim, Mary Wojtyla, sued the Burlington Northern Santa Fe. In 1996, the suit was dismissed. John Newell, an attorney representing the railroad, indicated that the trial court didn't believe this was an example of an unsafe crossing. There were no specific government safety regulations in place on how trains were to pass stopped trains in commuter stations, and it was left up to the individual railroads to make that determination. The train simply passed through a congested commuter station at close to seventy mph with a stopped train in the station. The BNSF broke no rules or special operating instructions and won the case.

As long as minimum required FRA and state safety regulations are met, the probability of a successful lawsuit against the BNSF remains low; however, the probability of a second-train incident at a commuter station crossing will continue to remain high.

Michael DeLarco

. . .

ONE FAMILY THAT HAS SPENT countless hours and significant sums of money working to improve railroad safety is the family of Michael DeLarco. The DeLarcos are a soft-spoken couple actively involved in the DuPage Railroad Safety Council. Whenever either Michael or Linda DeLarco speaks at a DRSC meeting, their comments are thoughtful and meaningful.

It was just minutes after six o'clock in the evening on February 23, 2004, when Linda DeLarco, her ten-year-old son, Michael, and eight-year-old daughter, Andreya, had detrained from an eastbound Metra/NIRC train at the Thatcher Avenue, River Grove, Illinois (DOT/AAR 372133T), commuter station.

Awaiting the family on the opposite side of the station's tracks was Linda's husband and young Andreya and Michael's father, also named Michael. The eastbound train was in the process of exiting the station. With only a red warning light flashing, and with no pedestrian warning gates at the crossing, young Michael saw his father on the opposite side of the tracks and began crossing. Young Michael was struck and killed by a high-speed westbound Metra/NIRC express train.

Michael and his father, as part of a Boy Scout adventure, were to spend the upcoming weekend sleeping on a submarine. Michael was an inquisitive boy who loved to read, often asked questions, and was a fifth grader at St. Hubert Catholic School in Hoffman Estates.

"I never saw him in a bad mood," said Grandmother Jackie DeLarco. "He just always had this smiling face."

A poem young Michael had written the week before, on February 20, was read at his memorial service. He called it "I Seem to Be" and wrote "I seem to be a fearsome tiger, but I am a gentle bird. I seem to be a radio, but I really am a peaceful ocean." (Peterson and Boykin, Family Grieves for Little Michael; Metra Continues to Investigate Death 2004)

"He was really a terrific kid, always smiling, never complaining," Michael's coach, Jim Murray, remembered. "His hustle and his heart were tremendous. If I had all of them like that, things would be easy." On November 21, 2004, after their first game of the season, St. Hubert Catholic School in Hoffman Estates retired his number fifty-four black and gold basketball jersey, and, since then, it has been displayed in a glass case outside the school gym. (Peterson, St. Hubert to Retire Jersey of Child Killed by a Train 2004)

The River Grove station is on the Metra Milwaukee District West Line. This line, like all but one of the other Metra lines, has special operating rules in place governing how and when trains can enter a station or pass through a station if another train is stopped in the station or in the process of exiting a station.

Special instruction 6.30 is the operating rule locomotive engineers operating on this line must follow. The rule establishes strict safety protocols on exactly when and how an approaching train can safely enter a station if there is a commuter train stopped in the station or in the process of exiting the station. The stopped commuter train also has a duty to remain in the station and protect pedestrians and commuters until it is safe to exit the station. Radio communications between the trains is a key element in determining how both trains will operate.

The locomotive engineer of the eastbound train was a student engineer who was working with an engineer with thirty years' experience, while the engineer of the westbound train had eight years' experience.

Metra spent two months investigating the accident before firing the three engineers in April 2004 for not following the railroad's special instruction 6.30. Additionally, proper radio communications between the two trains did not take place.

The November 2005 edition of "Locomotive Engineers and Trainmen News" tells how and why the three engineers were reinstated with back pay, and the efforts made on behalf of the engineers by the Brotherhood of Locomotive Engineers and Trainmen (BLET). The article states that a federal arbitrator ruled that Metra did not follow due process in firing the three. The BLET argued that

> a literal application of the rule did not require the eastbound train to remain stationary. The crew judged that their train would be well east of the station before the express train arrived, and that pedestrians about the station would be able to see and hear the express train approach, allowing them to take precaution to the train's passing. Instead, Metra argued that the engineers could have seen the express train sooner, before they had finished loading their passengers, and then the rule would have required that they stay stationary. The engineers testified that a headlight from an oncoming train prevented them from seeing the express train sooner."

BLET Vice-President Radek extended sincere sympathy to the family of Michael DeLarco and stated, "Many of us are parents, too, and we can all appreciate how difficult it is to cope with the loss of a child, regardless of the circumstances.

"We detected glaring inconsistencies in the level of safety accorded passengers on the various Metra lines," Radek said. "We have been working with state officials and with officials in the communities Metra serves to enhance the level of protection for pedestrians at train stations. Preventing another accidental death should be Michael DeLarco's legacy.

Eventually, after years of effort, Mike and Linda DeLarco were successful in their effort to make the River Grove crossing safer. The warning gate that had previously only provided protection for street traffic was moved in order to also protect the pedestrian sidewalk area. The platform was redesigned, and commuters are now channeled from the station platform to behind the warning gates prior to crossing the tracks. This was accomplished by cutting off a small portion of platform and putting in some inexpensive vertical tubing to act as a barrier guiding commuters to the area behind the downed warning gate.

Metra openly and almost immediately acknowledged that specific locomotive engineers' instructions were violated, and that these violations were a significant contributing factor leading to this River Grove incident. The main violation alleged by Metra was that the high-speed express train was allowed to pass through a congested station where another commuter train had just exited and that the exiting train should have remained in the station to protect those in the station until it was safe to exit.

The BNSF line is the one Metra rail line that allows high-speed commuter express trains to travel at almost seventy mph, Amtrak passenger trains travel at almost eighty mph, and freight trains at slower speeds to travel through congested stations when there are other stopped or exiting commuter trains at the station.

My office is less than two blocks north of the tracks in Downers Grove, and my home is south of the tracks. Either by foot or driving, I am typically at the Main Street crossing several times a day. What I have seen along the BNSF tracks is beyond scary.

The DeLarco family established a Foundation honoring young Michael, and it has helped support many different causes.

The Foundation's main purpose when formed was to raise funds in order to proceed with rail safety improvements to be implemented at the River Grove train station and crossing. The Foundation also supports various rail safety groups and projects.

The Michael S. DeLarco Foundation has always been a strong supporter of children and has granted wishes for the children that are associated with Make-A-Wish of Chicago, it has supported various activities at Michael's school, St. Hubert Catholic School, and has raised funds to sponsor a playroom with a library for children at The Alexian Brothers Women & Children's Hospital. The playroom has been named the Michael S. DeLarco Playroom and is a fun and calming space for the children who are patients at the Hospital.

When poor or no operating safety protocols are in place, the risk of second-train accidents occurring is far greater than when strict operating safety rules exist.

In 2011, Union Pacific, Metra, the Illinois Commerce Commission and the Illinois Department of Transportation redesigned many of its commuter stations along the UP West Line, in order to allow Metra and freight trains to enter a station when a commuter train is either stopped or exiting a station without having to follow special instruction 6.30 operating rules. In 2011, the Union Pacific installed and activated a new second-train pedestrian warning system at eight stations along their busy West Line. A press release (see previous chapter) announced the improvements and noted that second trains would now be allowed to pass through the stations without adhering to the hold out rule.

The redesigned stations now have both audible and visual signage that activates when a second train is in the area. A red "Danger!" sign begins flashing and a white "Another train coming" sign illuminates while a voice repeats: "Danger, another train coming." The station platforms also have been redesigned so that commuters and other pedestrians are forced to walk behind the warning gates.

At Metra commuter stations, with the exception of the Metra/BNSF line that has not yet been enhanced with these safety features, trains still must adhere to strict special instruction 6.30.

Northwestern University professor Ian Savage, a noted safety expert said, "I think some very low-tech and relatively inexpensive designs, such as channeling passengers off the platform away from a crossing, has big payoffs." (Wronski, Pedestrian Rail Alerts Updated 2011)

Passenger railroads with station platforms in multiple-track territory should work cooperatively to develop a standardized system to clearly and accurately communicate to passengers in station areas and on platforms that a second train (in addition to any train currently occupying or approaching any station track) is approaching the station and that its arrival may be obscured by the train in the station. Such a system should have both an audio and visual component, and its messages should be distinctive enough to attract attention in what may be a very busy and noisy environment. This system should be able to indicate tracks occupied, direction of travel, and whether any approaching train will stop at the station. (Wronski, Pedestrian Rail Alerts Updated 2011)

As of 2015, the BNSF continues to operate second trains through crowded commuter stations that do not have the enhanced second-train warning system. In fact, most people are not aware of the second train warning system that is in place. There is a lack of effort by both the BNSF and Metra to inform the general public as to how the active warning systems work.

Incident Reporting: Out of Sight, Out of Mind

. . .

When train collisions occur in Chicago and its suburbs, there often is little publicity beyond coverage in the local newspaper. On rare occasions, there might be a mention on TV or radio. Crossing incidents, especially those involving trains versus pedestrians, are too commonplace in Chicago and its suburbs to attract much attention. Too often they go almost unnoticed. Railroads are required to report train accidents to the Federal Railroad Administration within thirty days after the end of the month in which the collision occurred.

Based on these railroad accident reports, important statistical analysis is generated. These reports help determine just how safe a crossing is and whether existing safety measures at a specific crossing are adequate. The importance of the statistical reports cannot be minimized.

When I wrote to railroad safety expert Steve Laffey of the Illinois Commerce Commission about my concerns regarding trains passing stopped or exiting trains along the BNSF, he responded with a detailed spreadsheet indicating that there was only one fatal second-train commuter station crossing incident on the Metra/BNSF line over a nearly twenty-year period. The information was provided by the BNSF to the FRA through the railroad's responses contained in the accident/incident report form FRA F 6180.57 completed by the railroad. This report is used by the FRA to compile critical statistics used to manage risk. When reports are incomplete, incorrect, or misclassified, then risk will not be managed properly.

Risk-Based Hazard Analysis Approach to Enhancing Safety
FRA recommends that passenger rail operators use risk-based proactive hazard analysis methods to evaluate the risk associated with the movement of pedestrians at or near passenger stations, in light of the history of tragic incidents that have resulted in serious pedestrian injuries and fatalities. These unfortunate events have the potential to be reduced in number if the steps outlined in this document are applied using the risk-based hazard analysis process that takes into account the specific requirements and conditions of every passenger rail operation. (Federal Railroad Administration 2012)

Newspaper and police reports often give a much more accurate and different picture of how an accident occurs than many of the railroad accident reports I have reviewed.

When I told Steve Laffey of my concerns, he responded by indicating that none of the railroads do a really good job with the accident reports they provide. He went on to state that he has compared hundreds of police reports to the FRA required accident reports prepared by the railroads, and the differences were dramatic and very frustrating to resolve.

In a previous chapter of the book, I reviewed in some detail a relatively small number of accidents. Of those reviewed, most I first became aware of either through newspaper articles, radio or

TV newscasts, or the mention of the accident at one of our safety meetings.

Besides the differences between the railroad-prepared accident report forms 6180.57 when compared with the newspaper or police reports of railroad pedestrian accidents, there were several train-pedestrian fatal incidents that I was not able to find in the FRA accident/incident database. I again e-mailed Steve Laffey about my concerns. He indicated that form number 6180.57 "Highway-Rail Grade Crossing Accident/Incident Report" is for incidents that occur only at the intersection of the highway right-of-way and the railroad and that involve on-track rail equipment. If the railroad decides a specific accident does not fall into this category, a different form, 6180.55 "Railroad Injury and Illness," is used. It is up to the railroad to make the decision on how to classify the accident. Steve Laffey indicated that he was aware that incorrect reporting does take place and has worked with the FRA to correct specific misclassifications that he was aware of.

Train accident/incident analysis that is based on unreliable information leads to poor risk management.

A previous chapter listed some of the accidents I reviewed. Of those I reviewed, there were three that the railroads did not report on form 6180.57 "Highway-Rail Grade Accident/Incident Report" and were not reflected in accident/incident data prepared by the FRA. These are the Marie Niedziela, Scott Eskew, and Michael DeLarco accidents.

There was no Highway-Rail Grade Accident/Incident Report on file for the June 6, 1993, Fairview Avenue accident that had killed Marie Niedziela. The reason was because it was reported as a trespasser incident by the railroad and was reported on what is called a casualty report (6180.55a).

There was no Highway-Rail Grade Accident/Incident Report for the January, 23, 2004, accident that killed Scott Eskew in Berwyn on the BNSF line. The reason again was because it had been reported as a trespasser incident by the railroad and had been reported on a casualty report.

There was no Highway-Rail Grade Accident/Incident Report on file for the February 23, 2004, Michael DeLarco incident at River Grove on the Metra/NIRC. This had been reported as a non-trespasser and had been reported on a casualty report.

When I was drawn to these specific fatal incidents for one reason or another I would then look at a government supplied accident/incident database. These accidents were not in that database. Each of the three accidents further illustrates just how dangerous station crossings are.

In a 1995 newspaper article by Kevin M. McCarthy of the *Downers Grove Reporter,* "according to a[n] FRA report that predicts the possible number of accidents at a crossing based on previous incidents, the Fairview crossing ranked 35th most likely for accidents out of more than 10,000 crossings in Illinois." The article went on to say that "However, those records did not include one of the Fairview accidents in 1993. A federal official said he did not know why one of the accidents was not reported in the study." (McCarthy 1995)

Walt Bogdanich wrote a series of articles in 2004 that won a Pulitzer Prize. In one article titled "Death on the Tracks: A Crossing Crash Unreported and a Family Broken by Grief," he writes of the tragic death of seventeen-year-old Hilary Feaster on October 15, 1997. It was a clear day, but the overgrowth blocked the view of the tracks at the Highway 127 crossing in Decherd, Tennessee. Shortly after five o'clock in the evening, her car was struck by a thirty-four-car CSX freight train traveling at fifty-four mph. The crossing had no warning gates, and one of the crossing's two warning lights was not working.

It was only after Hilary Feaster's death, in a conversation with the mayor, that the Tennessee Department of Transportation became aware that four years earlier, in 1993, at the very same crossing, two teenage boys, Shilo Bush and Ryan Bush, were killed.

CSX had failed to report the earlier accident. If it had done so, the Tennessee Department of Transportation would have paid for the installation of warning gates prior to Hilary's death.

In the same *New York Times* July 12, 2004, article, the author writes "CSX's failure to report that first fatal crash may be its most serious reporting failure, but it is hardly an isolated omission. Over the last eight years, CSX and other railroads have failed to properly notify federal officials about hundreds of crossing accidents, according to federal records and a computer analysis of crash data by The New York Times." (Bogdanich, Death on the Tracks, A Crossing Crash Unreported and a Family Broken by Grief 2004)

When Changing
from the Usual

. . .

ONE SATURDAY, ON THE WAY back to Downers Grove after attending a monthly DRSC meeting in Hinsdale, I decided to take a westbound Metra/BNSF commuter train. There was some time before the westbound train was scheduled to arrive, so I decided to have breakfast at a restaurant across from the commuter station. As I walked to the restaurant, I noticed a large number of commuters waiting on the commuter platform on the south side of the tracks, which normally is meant for eastbound travelers heading inbound toward Chicago. The eastbound train was approaching on the north track, not the south track on which it would normally approach. With limited exceptions, inbound commuter trains stop at stations on the BNSF line using the south track, known as track three, and signage at the south station platform indicates that it is the platform side for inbound trains. Outbound trains typically use the north track, known as track one.

After my breakfast, I crossed the tracks to catch my outbound train, which would take me west to Downers Grove. My train was running late. New commuters had again gathered on the south side commuter platform to catch the next inbound train. Once again the inbound train, traveling east to Chicago, was using the north track. There was no announcement on the public address system at the station, but as passengers saw the approaching train they began running across the tracks in front of the nearby moving train from the south platform to the north platform, even as gates were down.

When I told the story at the next DRSC meeting, Tom Zapler, a retired railroad official, indicated that use of the opposite track by commuter trains is dangerous and has caused problems in the past. A common reason for commuter trains to use the nonassigned platform is track maintenance or freight traffic.

When commuter trains use the commuter platform on the opposite side of the tracks than what would be the assigned commuter platform, confusion among commuters often occurs. When it does happen, confused commuters, often because of poorly heard and understood announcements—or no announcement at all—run from one commuter platform to other. They seem oblivious to any of the dangers that exist.

On January 22, 2004, at 1:14 p.m., legally blind thirty-four-year-old Scott Eskew was struck and killed by a Metra/BNSF commuter train. Mr. Eskew consistently rode the 1:14 p.m. commuter train from Berwyn to Chicago in order to begin his job at three in the afternoon. His estate sued both the BNSF and Metra. Unlike many Metra accidents, which are settled before trial, this case went to trial. In 2009, a Cook County jury returned a verdict for the plaintiffs, the Eskew estate, in the amount of five million dollars, assigning 85 percent of the liability to the BNSF, 10 percent of the liability to Metra, and 5 percent contributory negligence to Eskew. The Illinois Supreme Court, in 2012, upheld the verdict.

According to excerpts from the Illinois Appellate Court's official report when the verdict was appealed:

Eskew was struck and killed by an eastbound commuter train as he attempted to cross from the platform on the north side of the tracks to the southern platform, where a 1:14 p.m. train usually arrived.

The 1:14 p.m. eastbound train to Chicago arrived on the southern track of the Berwyn station on 90% of its runs, and passengers regularly boarded the train from the southern platform. Occasionally, the eastbound train ran on the northern tracks, requiring passengers to board from the northern platform. On the date of the accident, the 1:14 commuter train was rerouted to the northern track due to an unexpected westbound freight train that was traveling on the center track.

Valerie Fitzgibbons, the BNSF station agent, testified she was informed of the track change for the commuter train just minutes before it was due to arrive. She made the two identical announcements to advise waiting passengers that the eastbound train to Chicago would board from the north rather than the south platform, stating "please cross over to the north platform." She made the first announcement before the freight arrived, and she made the second announcement when the freight train was passing through the station. Fitzgibbons acknowledged that she did not inform the waiting passengers that two trains were coming into the station, and was aware that announcements could not always be heard when a train is going by.

Several passengers testified that it was difficult to hear and understand the announcements on the north platform.

The plaintiffs presented expert testimony from Kenrick van Wyk, an acoustical engineer, who testified that, in his opinion, the passing freight train and the lack of speakers on the north side of the tracks interfered with the intelligibility of the announcements made over the public address system. Mr. van Wyk also expressed his opinion that, because the intelligibility of the announcement had been reduced, it was more likely than not that the message was confused, causing Eskew to cross the tracks. (Eskew v. Burlington Northern & Santa Fe Ry. Co. 2011)

It is now about ten years since the Scott Eskew incident. Commuter trains in the Metra system, from time to time, use the commuter platform on the opposite side at which it would normally be assigned to stop. Commuters are still often confused and scamper to the opposite side oblivious to whatever dangers exist on the tracks; public address communications are still often hard to hear or understand if there are any at all; and the risk of another Scott Eskew-type tragedy occurring is still far too high.

Unfunded Mandates

. . .

RAILROAD INCIDENTS OFTEN RESULT IN serious injury or death. About 25 percent of collisions result in a fatality, and another 25 percent cause injury. About 50 percent do not result in a fatality or injury. Train incidents have become commonplace in the Chicago area. Typically, the big papers such as the Tribune, Sun-Times, or Daily Herald pay little attention to most of the area railroad grade crossing collisions. A local suburban community paper will often give a more meaningful report.

Chicago is a railroad hub: about 25 percent of all freight traffic in the United States passes through it. Chicago is the only US city served by all six of the major freight rail lines. On a daily basis, there are about seven hundred commuter train movements, along with an additional five hundred freight and one hundred Amtrak movements. (Chicago's 21st Century Train Hub 2003)

There is a saying in railroading that, when the gates are down, to always expect a train. More often than not, that is true.

Two fairly recent train collisions captured the headlines of the major media. On December 19, 2007, at 2:54 p.m., 90-year-old Rose Tani drove around a stopped school bus and then around downed railroad warning gates at the Elizabeth Street grade crossing (DOT/AAR 174944W) in Lombard. She was killed when a freight train struck her car. This tragedy drew international attention, in large part, because her forty-six-year-old son Daniel Tani, an American astronaut, was orbiting the earth aboard the International Space Station and was not scheduled to return home until January 2008. He was notified by his wife and a flight surgeon who broke the news to him in a video conference call as he was orbiting earth. (Austin Peterson 2007)

Rose Tani's story is truly remarkable. During World War II, she spent more than two years in a Japanese American internment camps. At a memorial church service held shortly after her death, another son, Richard Tani, spoke of how he had recently seen a picture of himself as a toddler with his then twenty-five-year-old mother at a Utah Camp on a Ken Burns documentary called *The War*. Rose's husband had died when Daniel Tani was four years old. She had raised Daniel and his siblings alone. (Spak 2007)

According to witnesses on the school bus that saw the collision, Rose Tani was northbound and behind a school bus. Initially, the bus was stopped behind the downed gates and had approximately two other cars in front of it that were also stopped. The gates went up after an eastbound train passed; the vehicles in front of the school bus then crossed over the tracks, and then the gates went down when another train was approaching. The school bus was now the first vehicle stopped at the gates. Rose Tani drove around the stopped school bus and around the gates, and her Honda Civic was struck by a westbound freight train. (Illinois Traffic Crash Report LOMB-3-20071219-161712, Agency crash report No. 07-52753 2007)

We will never know what prompted Rose to drive around the downed gates. But there are more contributing factors to this story than just Rose Tani's driving around downed gates.

Tristian Hicks Williams will never share with her family the many joyful moments that Rose Tani was able to share with her family. On October 16, 2012, at about eight-fifteen in the morning, she drove around the activated railroad gates on 115th Street (DOT/AAR 608310D) near Marshfield Avenue in Chicago. Tristian Hicks Williams was twenty-six years old when a fast moving Metra Rock Island commuter train struck her van, resulting in her death. Tristian Hicks Williams was taking her two young sons, Jayvon, four, and JonKing, five, to Higgins Community Academy. Both children survived the collision but were seriously injured: Jayvon with injuries to his face, and JonKing with two broken legs.

Excerpts from a Chicago Tribune article by Jennifer Delgado, Bridget Doyle, and George Knue state, "Bill Williams stood on his front porch and waved to his wife and two little sons as they climbed into the family van on their way to school Tuesday, a weekday ritual. 'I told them I love them, have a good day at school, like I do every morning.' Williams said. And, 'I'll see you later.'"

Later in the same article, Tristian's sister Taja stated, "She was a wonderful mother, she loved her kids. They came first no matter what was going on in her life." The article goes on to state, "Records from the FRA show that five previous train-vehicle collisions have occurred at the same crossing since 1975. Each collision occurred after a motorist drove around the gate, officials said." The article continues "Metra spokeswoman Meg Reile said this is the 24th fatality involving Metra this year. All but four of these deaths have been pedestrians struck by trains, she said." (Delgado, Doyle and Knue 2012)

Like the Rose Tani collision, there are more contributing factors than just Tristian Hicks Williams's driving around downed gates.

There are almost 129,000 public railroad grade crossings in the United States. All but about twenty-nine hundred require that train horns be sounded. Federal regulations for mandatory train horn sounding, 49 CFR 222 and 229, require train horns to be sounded between fifteen and twenty seconds before a train enters the crossing. Although whistle posts are not required, they are a good idea and are often in place. When the train reaches the whistle post, which typically has a big *W* posted on it, the engineer sounds a series of prescribed whistle blasts, two long, one short, and one long. The whistle blasts continue until the train enters the crossing, for not less than fifteen seconds and not more twenty seconds.

Wikipedia

The crossings not requiring train horns to be blown are commonly known as "quiet zones." At these crossings, the train locomotive engineer does not typically sound the horn, but, at his discretion, will sound when he feels it is an emergency situation. At times, even in quiet zones, train horns are required to be sounded. Horns must be sounded 1) to warn roadway or track workers and 2) when passing the tail end of another train.

In Downers Grove, by my office, there are three crossings grouped together within less than half a mile. The Washington, Main, and Forest crossings are clustered together and are near the busy Main Street Train Station. Each crossing has a whistle ban or "quiet zone." However, these so called quiet zones are anything but quiet. Some trains sound their horns, and some trains do not. Some sound them when almost at the crossing in no systematic routine, and some well in advance of the crossing. Retired locomotive engineer Steve Frankowiak stated that he believed that the train horn should only be sounded when he observed a dangerous condition ahead.

When I took the Amtrak Southwest Chief in June 2015 from Kansas to Illinois, I timed the first sounding of the train horn until when I felt the locomotive first reached the crossing. It seemed to constantly be about eleven seconds. The sounding of the train horn at the whistle post, which is about a quarter mile from the crossing, will be shorter than the fifteen-to-twenty-second requirement with the faster Amtrak trains.

In the same 2003 report, the FRA also indicated that 407 of these "quiet crossings" were in Illinois. Most are in towns in the Chicago suburban area.

That said, it is important to note these two facts. Illinois is nearly always one of the three states with the highest number of railroad crossing collisions in the United States. Annually, train incidents in Chicago and its suburban area significantly add to the total number of railroad collisions in Illinois.

In 2003, the FRA reported that they had conducted a nationwide study that involved a large number of highway rail crossing collisions. The study determined that the likelihood of a railroad collision occurring at a "quiet-zone" crossing is 62 percent greater than at a gated crossing where train whistles are required to be blown. This study only confirmed earlier studies that showed that there is a much greater danger of a railroad/vehicle collision at a "quiet crossing." The most obvious reason is that the sooner someone realizes a train is approaching, the higher the likelihood that the person will not be impulsive and go around a downed gate.

In 1994, Congress passed and the president signed into law the Swift Rail Act that would require, at a future point in time, trains to blow whistles at all grade crossings, but would allow exceptions, or "quiet zones," to this whistle requirement if certain supplemental safety improvements were made to these crossings.

Almost every community in the Chicago region that had a quiet zone wanted to keep it. That is understandable. There are almost continuous crossings, there are many different rail lines, there are about fourteen hundred train movements daily, and they move twenty-four hours a day. This means millions of people would hear constant train whistles.

Communities argued that any changes to improve safety at an already quiet-zone crossing amounted to an unfunded mandate, and that local communities would have to bear the cost. They also argued that the value of the train horn in a dense urban area was questionable.

Although some of the improvements at the crossings may have cost little, or in fact no cost at all, the word "unfunded mandate" became the battle cry for community leaders and elected officials. Some were very heavy hitters in Congress.

There were meetings after meetings. Some I attended, and I, in fact, spoke or testified at several. The FRA gave examples of some improvements that would reduce the risk of collisions at crossings—any one of which would allow the crossing to remain as a "quiet zone."

The examples of added safety measures at a crossing included: raised medians in the roadway that would help to prevent a motorist from driving around a lowered gate, a four-quadrant gate system to block all lanes of highway traffic, converting a two-way street into a one way street, permanent closure of the crossing to highway traffic, the use of wayside horns posted at the crossing and directed at highway traffic only. The wayside horn localized the sound to the immediate vicinity of the crossing. (FRA Train Horn Rule Fact Sheet 2006)

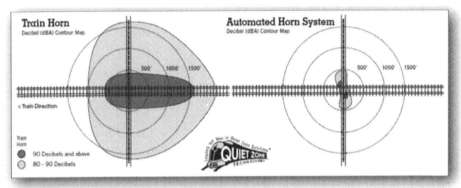

Figure on left: horn sounded from train; figure on right: sounded at crossing

Medians seemed doable for some crossings, and at a very low cost. However, at others you would have to reconstruct the street and move existing devices. The median strip would be an elevated strip or some type of vertical barrier running down the middle of the highway for about one hundred feet, separating the lanes in advance of the downed gate. The barrier would prevent vehicles from going around the gates, or from going around vehicles stopped at the gates.

Traffic lights on southbound South Garfield Street at the intersection with West Front Avenue and the incline leading to grade crossing.

The arguing went on for years, with the FRA holding off on their final regulations until the FRA published the final rule in 2005, and all the while allowing "quiet zones" to remain "quiet zones" with no supplemental safety measures put in place.

Finally, the FRA's Final Rule on the use of Locomotive Horns at Highway/Rail Grade Crossings became effective June 24, 2005. Quiet zones in the six county Chicago region of Cook, DuPage, Lake, Kane, McHenry and Will Counties that were in existence as of December 18, 2003, were exempted from the FRA's final rule and remained under jurisdiction of the Illinois Commerce Commission (ICC). A total of 399 quiet crossings were exempted.

In other words, a preexisting quiet crossing with active warning gates in the Chicago Region would remain quiet without requiring that an additional supplemental or alternative safety measure be added. According to existing Illinois regulations, if three or more collisions occurred in a five-year period at a specific crossing, then train whistles would be required to be blown at that crossing.

Some of the 399 ICC exempt rail crossings added these additional supplemental or alternative safety measures anyway, but most did not. The Chicago Region remains one of the most railroad-incident-prone areas in the United States.

The Union Pacific Railroad published on their website a page called "Federal Railroad Administration's Train Horn & Quiet Zone Rule." The page reads in part, "Union Pacific believes quiet zones compromise the safety of railroad employees, customers and the general public. While the railroad does not endorse quiet zones, it does comply with the provisions outlined in the federal law. Federal regulations provided public authorities the option to maintain and/or establish quiet zones provided certain supplemental or alternative safety measures are in place and the crossing collision rate meets

FRA standards." Again, in the Chicago Region there are 399 crossings that are exempt from these federal regulations. There have been many new quiet crossings in the Chicago Region that have been established since the exception date. They now meet the FRA "reasonable exception" guidelines and have an enhanced safety measure.

Are "quiet-zone" crossings significantly safer than crossings that require whistle blowing?

In some parts of the country that may be true. But according to statistics provided by Steve Laffey, in the seven-county area that includes Chicago, there was no meaningful difference in the number of railroad/highway crashes over the ten-year period of 2001 through 2010 when comparing incidents occurring in "quiet zones" versus those not in quiet zones.

In three collisions, the Fox River Grove school bus, the Midland Heroes' Parade, and an Amtrak collision in Mirian, Nevada (not reviewed in this book), the NTSB indicated that the vehicle drivers did not hear or recognize the train horn. Either soundproofing in the vehicle or ambient background noises were listed as the reason. In two other collisions, Bourbonnais and University Park, the train's event recorder indicated the train horn was sounded about fifteen seconds before the crash, but witnesses stated they did not hear the horn or implied that, when they did hear it, it was too late to react.

Rose Tani and Tristian Hicks Williams were killed at Chicago-area quiet-zone grade crossings exempted from federal regulation. It would have been difficult for either Rose Tani or Tristian Hicks Williams to go around downed gates if either the median lane divider or four-quadrant gates had been installed.

Supplemental safety measures save lives and should be considered at all railroad grade crossings.

Tragedy on the Tracks

. . .

Fox River Grove, October 25, 1995

WE SOON FOUND OUT HOW IMPORTANT SECONDS AND INCHES WERE.
WEDNESDAY MORNING, OCTOBER 25, 1995, was crisp and clear in the little town of Fox River Grove, Illinois. Parents were saying their good-byes to sleepy-eyed kids as they shut doors and the kids trotted off to the school bus stop. This small, bedroom community about forty miles northwest of Chicago is nestled along the scenic Fox River, which gave the town its charming and alluring name.

Lynn Thames, the regular school bus driver for Cary-Grove High School bus route No. 608, had taken the morning off to care for her sick son. Ms. Thames had called in at about five-thirty that morning to notify her employer that she would not be in. The substitute, Patricia Catencamp, was an experienced driver, but had never driven route 608 before. As might be expected with a driver unfamiliar with the route, the bus was running late. She was provided with a route map, did her pretrip inspection of the bus, and departed the bus garage at 6:35 a.m., which was twenty minutes later than the regular departure time. As students waited for the tardy bus to arrive, family members gathered some of them up and drove them to school, but most waited. (Walsh, 5 Die When Train Hits School Bus 1995)

At 7:10 a.m., life in Fox River Grove would tragically change, never to be the same again.

As I listened to WGN on the car radio, a report came in of a train hitting a school bus just minutes earlier. A former cop-turned-roving-radio-reporter, Larry Schreiner, was at the scene. Now twenty years later, I can still remember the tone in his voice as he approached the bus. There was little emotion. This hard-nosed beat reporter had seen much throughout his career. As he approached the school bus, it appeared that there was little damage, and he gave the impression that the collision wasn't serious. Within seconds, as he walked to other side of the bus, the matter-of-fact reporting suddenly changed. Schreiner's voice suddenly was filled with emotion. Over many years of hearing him on the radio, I had never heard this heartfelt emotion in his voice. It was hard for him to talk. Kids were lying everywhere, many dead or dying, and many injured. There was a feeling of helplessness in his voice. A school bus that just minutes earlier had been filled with kids and a driver, now laid shattered with the body of the bus shredded off its chassis.

Figure 2 – accident scene

The collision was almost as bad as it could get. The yellow school bus had been about half full, carrying thirty-five high school students. Some kids had been listening to radios, at least one was sleeping, and others were talking and laughing. That all changed when their bus was struck by a high-speed Metra/UP commuter train.

Nurse Helen Getchell had stopped for coffee at a convenience store across the street from the collision site. She immediately ran to the scene, where she used a turkey baster from the store to frantically suction blood from the throat of an injured boy. "It was frustrating; I didn't have the equipment," she said. "He died in my arms. I want to tell the mother that he didn't die alone. I held him in my arms, I was there." (Walsh, 5 Die When Train Hits School Bus 1995)

Within the blink of an eye, this scenic little community became the focus of all our prayers. We immediately knew it was going to be bad, and we soon found out just how bad. The front-page photo of Kimberly Schneider in the next day's Chicago Sun-Times reflected the agony of a mother as she waited for word about her daughter, Tiffany. She was soon to learn that Tiffany had been fatally injured. In total, seven Cary-Grove High School students would die, and twenty-eight more were injured.

Within days, we all learned how dangerous railroad grade crossings are in Illinois—and that the Fox River Grove crossing was one of the most dangerous. We soon found out how important seconds and inches were when it came to life or death. We were told about the many contributing factors that came together at one moment in time. To eliminate or change any one of these contributing factors could reduce the likelihood of future similar collisions from occurring.

It was the second time I had heard live commentary from a train collision scene. The first time, I was in the back of an ambulance being rushed to a hospital. That time, the only thing I knew about railroad safety was that when the gates go down, a train is approaching.

This time it was different. Immediately, I began to consider what some of the contributing factors might be.

It is my opinion that some significant contributing factors were never noted by the National Transportation Safety Board (NTSB). There is an old adage to "look for the obvious." Nearly nineteen years after the collision, I am convinced the NTSB both ignored and missed some of the obvious and important contributing factors:

* Metra/UP commuter express train 624, a push/pull train, was traveling eastbound toward Chicago's loop at about sixty-nine miles per hour when it slammed into the back of the school bus. The impact was so great it turned the frame of the bus by 180 degrees, so that the front of the body of the bus was now facing the track and the front of the chassis was facing the opposite direction. The train, as is the case with all commuter trains traveling inbound to Chicago, was being pushed by a locomotive. The locomotive engineer was Ford Dotson Jr., and he controlled the train from a compartment at the front of the lead eastbound passenger car. It is called the control cab. This push-pull system is how Metra commuter trains operate: the locomotive pulls the trains outbound from Chicago and then pushes the train inbound to Chicago.

* Pictures of the inbound control cab car twin headlight appeared in the paper. As with the Elmhurst accident that had occurred exactly one year to the day earlier, this control cab car had only the one twin headlight centered and set high. There was no distinctive and recognizable triangular lighting system that the Metra locomotives displayed when they pull trains from Chicago to its suburbs.

* The Algonquin Road (DOT/AAR 176958L) grade crossing, where the collision occurred, sits just one block southeast and

on the same set of tracks as the Lincoln Road (DOT/AAR 176959T) grade crossing. Prior to this train-versus-school-bus collision, there had been many collisions at each of these two railroad grade crossings. Since 1929, these two crossings had a combined total of twenty-seven train-related collisions resulting in fifteen fatalities. Just weeks earlier, on September 18, 1995, at 7:07 a.m., there had been another collision at Algonquin Road, when the same Metra express commuter train, 624, had struck a truck. (Janov and Rozek 1995)

* Without dramatic safety improvements, the probability of another train collision occurring at this intersection was high. Exactly the opposite of safety improvements took place. In 1990, this already dangerous crossing was made even more dangerous. The collision occurred immediately after the school bus had crossed the two-tracks at the Algonquin Road grade crossing and stopped for a red light at Algonquin Road and Northwest Highway. Northwest Highway, also known as Route 14, is the intersecting road that runs parallel to the tracks.

About five years earlier, in 1990, Northwest Highway had been widened from a twenty-four-foot, two-lane highway to a sixty-foot, five-lane highway. In the process, the storage distance, or queue length, between the railroad tracks and Northwest Highway was decreased by thirty-six feet. The length of the street for northbound Algonquin Road traffic crossing the tracks went from sixty-six feet, six inches to thirty feet, six inches. The length of the school bus was thirty-eight feet, four inches. When the northbound school bus went over the railroad tracks and stopped at the red light, the rear end of the bus extended seven inches over the northern track. (Washburn, Gibson and Martin 1995)

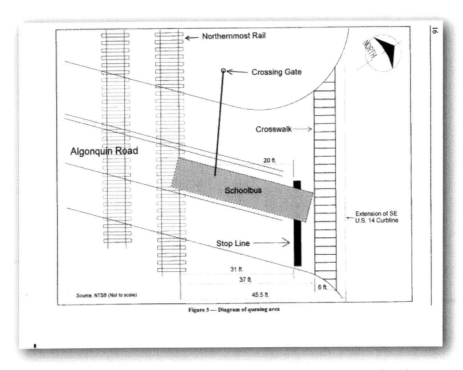

Figure 5 — Diagram of queuing area

Experienced bus drivers later testified that, on this school route, they would wait south of the tracks for the light to turn green before proceeding across the tracks to the intersection. Patricia Catencamp, running this route for the first time, did not. She had not been instructed to do so. When she stopped at the light, she mistakenly thought the bus had completely cleared the tracks.

The approaching Metra/UP express, traveling at about one hundred feet per second, tripped a sensor at 3,080 feet from the crossing. Once the sensor was tripped, it was set to calculate the train's speed, which in turn would start the warning-gate cycle at the crossing and at the same time, the cycle of signal changes for the traffic light at Algonquin Road and Northwest Highway was set to begin. The traffic light was supposed to be green for northbound traffic on Algonquin Road prior to the train arriving. When the light on northbound Algonquin Road was green vehicle traffic would hopefully move forward and any vehicles caught on the tracks would be able to clear the tracks. Warning lights at the crossing would activate, and seconds later, crossing gates would begin going down. Although NTSB investigators came up with slightly different results, they felt that the crossing-gate-warning sequence and the traffic-signal sequence both began about twenty seconds before the collision.

As the eastbound Metra/UP commuter train approached the crossing at almost seventy mph, the locomotive engineer testified he saw the bus slowly crossing the tracks at about twenty-three hundred feet, or about twenty-three seconds from the crossing. He stated he was crossing over the Fox River Bridge when he first saw the slowly moving bus. Did the school bus cross the tracks and then sit at a red light, with its rear extending slightly over the track, for about twenty seconds before the collision? This is what the NTSB concluded.

The NTSB provided a seating chart of where the students on the school bus had sat just prior to the collision, and, if they had moved, where to. The chart also indicated whether that student had been killed or injured. All of the students that were fatally injured were sitting in the back four rows of the bus. Just before impact, a couple of students in the back of the bus recognized that the train was approaching and managed to move forward just a few feet. They survived. The bus driver stated she had stopped before crossing the tracks, and then looked down the tracks but did not see the train approaching.

A train approaching with just one twin headlight set high and centered would be difficult to recognize as an approaching train, especially when there is a background of high set fixed lighting at the station and on street lamp posts. This train, at that distance, as was the one involved in the Elmhurst incident that occurred exactly one year earlier, would have been almost indistinguishable to anyone at the crossing.

Two days after the collision, John Goglia of the NTSB calculated that the driver had only two seconds to react before the light had turned red, following a twelve-second Don't Walk sign on Algonquin Road, a 4.5-second transition from yellow to red on Northwest Highway traffic light, and a 1.5-second red to green transition on Algonquin Road traffic light. "If it takes 18 seconds for the light to turn green, and the train is going to cross in 20, I'm not comfortable. That simply is not enough time for a human being to recognize that a light has changed, take your foot off the brake, and move out of the way. I'm troubled by the timing sequence," Goglia said. (Rozek and McKinney 1995)

The NTSB final report, "Highway/Railroad Accident Report NTSB/HAR-96/02, PB 96-916202," adopted October 29, 1996, on the Fox River Grove train collision with the school bus states:

"The Federal Highway Administration (FHWA) Railroad/ Highway Grade Crossing Handbook states: On tracks where trains operate at speeds of 20 mph or higher, the circuits controlling automatic light signals shall provide for a minimum operation of 20 seconds before the arrival of any train. The 20-second warning time is a minimum."

A UP representative testified at the Safety Board's public hearing in January 1996 that "we design our circuits for 25 seconds to give a 5 second buffer...because there are conditions out on the track that make us unable to give an exact warning time. These conditions are beyond our control, and we know that this warning time is going to fluctuate, so we put in a 5 second buffer to this 20 seconds."

Kirk Brown, Secretary of the Illinois Department of Transportation, said, "If a train's going 69 miles an hour, we need more than 20 seconds of advanced warning."

Maintenance records released by the state showed 10 complaints since January of that year about the Algonquin Road-Northwest

Highway traffic signal. At least seven were related to the synchronization of the stoplight and the railroad warning gates. (McKinney, 10 signal complaints tallied in '95 1995)

Coincidentally, Fox River Grove Police Chief Robert Polston and Bob McWilliams of the Illinois Department of Transportation were at the crossing that morning to investigate the signal complaints and both witnessed the collision.

The state immediately began inspecting similar rail-grade crossings for signal design problems. As media reports soon indicated, the probability of this type of collision occurring had been high for many years and was due to a number of contributing and predictable factors:

* The short time sequence of the traffic signals was well noted, and both the Lincoln and Algonquin grade crossings had histories of collisions, yet the train was traveling through the grade crossing at the maximum allowable speed.
* The space between the white stop line at the traffic light and the tracks was not long enough for the school bus to safely fit. Five years earlier there would have been plenty of room.
* Due to a lack of communication, the substitute driver didn't know standard operating procedures at the crossing and proceeded to cross tracks while there was a red light showing at the intersection of Algonquin Road and Northwest Highway. The regular driver would have waited before crossing the tracks and proceeded only when the light at Algonquin and Northwest Highway turned green.

The NTSB quickly made recommendations it believed necessary to improve safety. The NTSB's published recommendations are widely distributed and have a major influence in the transportation industry.

This is a critically important point that I will make over and over again: if the NTSB, or for that matter, the FRA, does not do a good job in its investigative process, and significant contributing factors go unnoticed, transportation safety suffers.

It took about a year for the NTSB to issue its final report on the Fox River Grove train–school bus collision. In my opinion, the agency failed to note some very significant contributing factors.

Why was there a difference in the timeline as to when the loco-motive engineer thought he had begun reacting to the bus moving across the tracks—about twenty-three seconds from the crossing—and when he actually *did* react, about ten seconds from the crossing? That difference has troubled me for years. If the NTSB had explored this timeline difference and reached the same conclusion I have, rail safety may have improved not only in Illinois, but nationally.

The NTSB seldom investigates highway-rail incidents, in contrast to aviation incidents, where they investigate all crashes. According to the FRA, there were 4,633 highway-rail incidents in 1995. The NTSB database reflects that it investigated just two of these 1995 highway-rail incidents. A train collision has to be considered a major event for the NTSB to investigate. If correctable contributing factors are missed, they may go unnoticed in future train collisions that do not undergo an NTSB investigation.

The FRA is also empowered to investigate railroad accidents but seldom does. For example, in 2003 there were nearly 3,000 rail crossing accidents, but the FRA only investigated four. (W. Bogdanich, J. Nordberg and t. Torok, et al. 2004)

The lobby at the Holiday Inn in Crystal Lake, Illinois, was empty when I arrived at about three o'clock in the morning. The Midwest is known for its cold winters, and January 19, 1996, was a bone chilling day. It was the last of the three days of hearings that the NTSB was holding on the Fox River Grove train–school bus collision.

Soon after the collision, I had traveled to the collision site. The track was straight with a good line of sight. Why didn't the experienced school bus driver and the students realize a train was approaching and react sooner? We learned early on from the NTSB that they believed the warnings at the crossing activated about twenty seconds prior to the collision. The stopped bus was struck by the downward movement of the warning arm as it waited for the red light to change.

The locomotive engineer later testified that he first saw the school bus as it was slowly crossing the tracks when he was about twenty-three hundred feet from the crossing. If the warning signals had activated in a timely manner, that would have been about twenty-three seconds before the collision. There was either no reaction or delayed reactions by the students in the bus, and no reaction by the bus driver.

Although I had not planned on attending the hearings and did not for the first two days, I was drawn there on that third and final day. After lying in bed tossing and turning for some time, I decided to go to the hearing. I had something to say and I wanted to be heard. The Holiday Inn in Crystal Lake was about 50 miles from where I lived and my brain was racing all over the place as I drove there.

As I waited in the empty hotel lobby at that early hour, two men sat down near me. My ears perked up as they started talking about the collision. After listening for a time, I approached them and learned they were with the NTSB. Immediately, I began talking about how much safer commuter trains are that use the enhanced triangular lighting pattern than those that do not.

I also told them about the fatal Elmhurst incident a year earlier when a Metra/UP control cab car with just a single twin headlight struck and killed a pedestrian after leaving the station a half mile west of this station. I was there the next morning at exactly the same time, and with all the lighting in the station, it was difficult for me to recognize the train in the station even though I knew it was there.

At the time, freight train locomotives traveling throughout this country were equipped with one head light located and centered high on the front end on the locomotive and it was always lit. However, the freight train locomotives that I observed also had a set of ditch lights that sat low to the ground on each side of the locomotive. It made no difference whether it was day or night; these ditch lights, based on my many hours of observing freight trains on the BNSF and UP lines, seemed *never* to be lit. As a result, there was no triangular pattern in front of the train to help alert someone down the tracks that a train was approaching. The sooner someone recognizes that a train is approaching, the sooner that person can react. This is basic common sense. **Mere inches and seconds can mean the difference between life and death.**

In the year between the accidents in Elmhurst and Fox River Grove, I expressed my concerns to anyone who I thought could help bring about change, including Federal Railroad Administration Administrator Jolene Molitoris. In response, Ms. Molitoris indicated that all trains operating at speeds over twenty mph would be required by regulation to have the three-light triangular system on all locomotives and control cab cars lit whenever operating. But that requirement would not become effective until December 31, 1997. In 1992, the federal regulation only **recommended** that these lights be used; it would not become mandatory until the 1997 date.

The big freight lines that I observed, the BNSF and UP, for whatever reason, were choosing not to use their ditch lights. One safety expert indicated that he believed the Norfolk Southern had operated their trains during this period with the ditch lights on.

As I talked to the two NTSB investigators in that Holiday Inn lobby, I presented my argument about the train lighting and asked if I could testify about my concerns at Friday's hearing. NTSB Investigator George Cochran indicated that the NTSB hearings were very structured and all witnesses had been scheduled. I would not be allowed to testify.

As I attended the hearing, much of the testimony seemed to go in one ear and out the other. My thoughts kept turning to the lighting on the control cab car. Collisions continued to take place, and too many people were dying as a result of these poorly lit lead control cab cars. Better lit Metra locomotives on all their lines, and better lit Metra control cab cars on the BNSF line, were involved in fewer collisions.

The school bus driver had not seen the distant train approaching as she started across the tracks, yet the locomotive engineer saw her. She had stopped before the crossing, opened the bus door and looked both right and left, but she didn't see the train. She proceeded across to the north side of the tracks and stopped at the red light, thinking her bus had cleared the tracks. She was wrong.

During a break in the hearing, the NTSB's George Cochran came up to me and handed me a document. The document, "Locomotive Visibility: Minimum Standards for Auxiliary Lights," released by the Federal Railroad Administration's Office of Safety on July 25, 1995. When I read the document later that day, I was floored. It was a well-researched report that was prepared by the prestigious Volpe National Systems Center. At about thirty pages in length, the report ended with the following estimated twenty-year benefits. "Expected reductions in accidents 6,300; fatalities 1,493; injuries 3,056." All that had to be done was to make the lead car of the train more recognizable through lighting—exactly what I had been calling for, for more than a year. Recognition of and reaction to potential danger is important.

When the NTSB issued its final report, it went into great detail about the many contributing factors to the collision. "He (Dotson) said he saw the bus cross the tracks in front of him. If he could see the bus, why couldn't she (Catencamp) see the train?" said Cathy Kalte whose son, Joe, died in the accident. (Dungey, Janov and Minor 1996)

In late 1996, I sent a published op-ed letter I had written earlier about the importance of triangular lighting, along with excerpts of the "Locomotive Visibility: Minimum Standards for Auxiliary Lights" report to the CEOs of all the major Class 1 freight carriers in the United States.

The letter also included a graphic of a wise owl sitting on a branch with this suggestion: "You can make this Christmas brighter and safer for everyone. Most locomotives are equipped with some type of safety light system (i.e., ditch, crossing, or oscillating). These lights, when on, make trains more conspicuous and, in turn, much safer. Please ask your engineers to use them 24 hours a day. Best wishes for a happy holiday season."

Within two weeks the freight lines started turning on their ditch lights, creating that triangular pattern. They remain on night or day, whenever a train is in operation.

Many years after the lights went on, I attended a presentation by a railroad safety expert. He showed how railroad accidents had started to dramatically decrease beginning in 1997.

When I asked the presenter if he had any idea as to why, he said it was the ditch-light effect. When trains turned on their ditch lights, the triangular lighting took effect, and people recognized the approaching train, and accidents went down.

In 1998, there were 3,508 highway-rail incidents according the FRA. In 2009 there were 1,925 highway-rail incidents. In twelve years, there had been over a 40 percent decrease in highway-rail incidents. (Railroad Safety Statistics-Annual Report 2009-Final 2011)

The NTSB was aware of the importance of recognizable lighting on locomotives and control cab cars by January 19, 1996. That was when NTSB's George Cochran gave me the report. The NTSB final report of the Fox River Grove train–school bus collision missed important contributing factors; the lack of recognizable lighting on the control cab car was just one.

There were other issues not addressed by the NTSB. One was redundancy, or two man crews. In transportation safety, redundancy is a key concept. Commercial airlines have two pilots, the landing system may be lowered either through hydraulics or manually, and Class I freight railroad carriers have a locomotive engineer and a conductor in the locomotive compartment, each capable of stopping the train, calling out signal aspects to the other, or alerting the other of danger.

At a November 1–2, 1995, symposium on operator fatigue, held about a week after the Fox River Grove Collision, Department of Transportation Secretary Federico Peña commented, "Human factors cause a third of all railroad collisions and are the number one cause in aviation collisions...

The danger from fatigue is not just someone will nod off or sleep at the controls of a plane, ship, train or motor vehicle, although I'm sure all of those have happened. The insidious danger is that the operator may become dulled enough to miss—or misinterpret—a critical danger signal, or be slow in responding to it." (Peña 1995)

As with any collision investigation, a timeline of the events is important. This can be done in several ways. Testimony of witnesses and those involved in the collision will shed some light. A re-creation of the chain of events leading up to the actual colli-sion would be helpful. A camera or other equipment that recorded events in real time would be of great importance. The NTSB used all three to establish its timeline from when the engineer first saw the big, yellow school bus on the tracks and then first started to react, and when the train finally came to a complete stop.

There was testimony from many: those involved in the collision, bus drivers familiar with the route but not on the scene of the colli-sion, witnesses at the scene of the collision, and others.

There was a detailed review of the train's event recorder. The event recorder is a device on the train that records data about the operation of the train and its performance. It is used to record time, distance, speed, brake pipe pressure, throttle position, emergency brake application, etc. and is similar to a black box on a plane gives in that it records information.

There were stopping tests using the accident train traveling at about seventy mph, and using the accident train's event recorder in-formation to replicate when the train began to reduce speed, began stopping, and the distance it took to stop.

There are serious discrepancies in the timeline between when locomotive engineer Ford Dotson Jr. first thought he began reacting to the school bus and when he actually did react.

Dotson testified that he first saw the school bus moving slowly across the tracks as he crossed the Fox River Bridge, at about twenty-three hundred feet west of Algonquin Road. The train was travel-ing at about sixty-nine mph or about one hundred feet per second. When engineer Dotson first saw the bus, it was about twenty-three seconds before the collision.

Dotson testified at the NTSB hearing, "and the next thing I would be looking for would be Algonquin Road. But this particular morning, I would say about the time I came off the bridge, this is when I noticed the bus crossing track No. 1. It was just about to cross track one when I noticed it. The first thing that came to my mind is, 'this bus is moving awfully slow.' At this time, I don't know if it's going to stop or if it's going to keep going."

At this point, NTSB investigator Cochran asked, "Do you recall what you next did when you saw the bus?"

Engineer Dotson responded "Moving at the speed it was, my first instinct was to drop my throttle and set my brakes. This is what I did. Just about the time I set them up, I put it in emergency. And at the same time, I was whistling. I started whistling signal 15L, which is two longs, a short and a long. After whistling 15L, just about this time the bus came to a stop with its hind end hanging out over track No. 2 the track that I'm on. I didn't know why it stopped." (Engineer Follows Instincts, But Can't Stop in Time 1996)

The train's event recorder indicated a much different timeline. The following is taken from the NTSB final report:

The on-scene event recorder readout by the UP indicates that the throttle was moved from its maximum "8" to "idle" at a calculated distance between 965 and 1,066 feet west of the crossing. About 2 seconds later, a full-service brake application was made at a calculated distance between 762 and 864 feet west of the crossing. The speed of the train during the throttle change and the full-service brake application was about 69 mph. About 2 seconds later, an emergency brake application was made at a calculated distance between 661 and 762 feet west of the crossing, when the train was traveling about 67 mph. Impact with the school bus occurred about 5 seconds later, when the train was traveling about 60 mph. (Board, Highway/Railroad Accident Report NTSB/HAR-96/02, PB 96-916202 1996)

Within days after the collision, the NTSB performed stopping-distance tests using the same train involved in the collision. Investigators replicated the conditions as closely as possible, such as the position change of the throttle and the full-service and emergency brake applications. The tests were conducted with the collision train traveling seventy mph, the position change of the throttle, and the full-service brake applications. The tests confirmed the reliability of the on-scene initial event recorder data.

The event recorder indicated the train was first placed in idle at about ten to eleven seconds west of the crossing, then full-service brakes were applied about nine seconds west of the crossing, and two seconds later, an emergency brake application. Mr. Dotson testified that the bus was moving when he placed the train in idle and initiated the emergency stop. If his testimony on this point is correct, and the warnings at the crossing had not yet begun activation when the bus began crossing, then the NTSB report is incorrect when it states that the warning system began activation about twenty seconds before the train entered the crossing.

The red light at Algonquin Road kept the school bus from proceeding onto Northwest Highway. Within several days of the collision, John Goglia of the NTSB indicated that a flaw with the traffic warning system was a contributing factor. The flaw allowed some trains to reach the Algonquin Road crossing within twenty seconds of tripping the track circuit mechanism that starts changing the traffic-signal light from red to green. It takes eighteen seconds for the light to actually turn green at Algonquin Road once the sequence starts with a pedestrian Don't Walk sign. That leaves only *two seconds* for drivers to react to a green light and move their vehicles off the crossing.

"That simply is not enough time for a human being to recognize the light has changed, take the foot off the brake and put it on the accelerator and move out of the way," Goglia told the *Chicago Sun-Times*. (Jimenez and Brown 1995)

What could cause such a significant discrepancy between the locomotive engineer's impression of the collision and what actually occurred? Could operator fatigue have been a contributing factor? Not according to the NTSB. But a closer look at engineer Ford Dotson Jr.'s sleep patterns preceding the Fox River Grove collision seems to point to fatigue as a contributing factor. The following timeline from the NTSB's final report tells of Dotson's long work hours, his extended drive to and from work, and his unusual sleep patterns:

Saturday, October 21: Engineer Dotson was off duty on Saturday. He awoke on Saturday about 9 a.m. and spent the majority of the day painting his home. He said that he stopped painting as darkness fell and then watched TV. He went to bed Saturday night between 9 and 10 p.m.

Sunday, October 22: The engineer repeated the same schedule as Saturday, continuing his painting.

Monday, October 23: The engineer worked the same job assignment and schedule Monday through Friday. He began his work week on Monday when he got up between 4 and 4:15 a.m. to get ready for work. He left home shortly after 5 a.m. and reported for duty in Crystal Lake between 6:25 a.m. and 6:30 a.m., after a one hour and 20 minute drive.

He left Crystal Lake on Train 624 to Chicago, arriving at 8:24 a.m. He then took the train to the coach yard for cleaning and the engine to a separate yard for refueling. He finished these tasks between 9:15 and 9:30 a.m. He then got breakfast and went to a nearby facility to sleep. The facility has bunk beds set up by the railroad to accommodate crew members on long layovers. He slept for 4 hours.

The engineer reported back to duty at 3:15 p.m. He picked up an engine and coaches and left Chicago on Train 341 at 5:21 p.m. en route to Winnetka, Illinois, which is on the CNW North line. He made all 10 stops on his way north, arriving at Winnetka at 5:54. He changed operating ends of the train and left Winnetka a couple of minutes after 6 p.m. He had to make only two stops returning to Chicago and arrived there at 6:30 p.m.

From 6:30 until 7:30 p.m., the engineer was off duty again. He used the time to eat dinner. At 7:30 p.m., he left Chicago operating Train 655 back to Crystal Lake and arrived at 8:53 p.m. He went off duty at 9:25 to 9:30 p.m. and made the one hour, 20 minute drive home, arriving at about 10:50 p.m. He ate a dinner his wife had already prepared for him and watched TV. He fell asleep before 11:30 p.m.

Tuesday, October 24: The engineer reported he kept the same schedule and activities, including sleep time on Tuesday.

Wednesday, October 25: The engineer again got up between 4:15 and 4:30 a.m. and arrived at work about 6:30 a.m. The collision occurred at 7:11 a.m. Consequently, by the time of the collision, the engineer had been on duty for approximately 45 minutes, and awake for approximately 3 hours. His most recent sleep period had been about five hours and he had nine hours of sleep in the previous 24 hours.

A person's quantity of sleep is hard to monitor, and their quality sleep time is almost impossible to monitor. Self-testimony, although somewhat meaningful, should not be the final determining factor as to whether operator fatigue was a contributing factor.

In July 2012, I met with Dennis Mogan. Mr. Mogan, a former locomotive engineer, was Metra's Director of Safety and Rules at the time of the collision. He was also a member of the Fox River Grove collision investigation team that was assembled by the NTSB. I mentioned that Dotson had stated he went to a railroad rest facility equipped with bunk beds and slept for four hours during his split-shift time off. Mogan looked surprised and stated that those facilities are not really meant for restful sleeps, in fact they were not really conducive to sleep at all. (Mogan 2012)

Locomotive Engineer Steve Frankowiak stated that the FRA does not require beds or even a sleep area for train crews.

Shortly after receiving a copy of the NTSB's final report on the Fox River Grove collision, I wrote NTSB Chairman Jim Hall about concerns I had with it. While the NTSB accident report mentioned various contributing factors, it did not mention several significant contributing factors, including operator fatigue on the part of the locomotive engineer and the lack of enhanced triangular lighting on the train's control cab car. Both were significant, in my opinion, and both should have been indicated in the report.

Hall responded in detail to my letter. "Your comments concerning possible fatigue in the engineer were quite perceptive," he wrote. "However, the safety board's investigation concluded that the engineer's actions were appropriate and that his observation of the school bus and actions to slow the train showed that he was alert. Consequently, there is no evidence that his performance was affected by fatigue resulting from lack of sleep. While the safety board could not justify fatigue as a contributing factor in this collision, it did consider the engineer's split work shift and the time in traveling to and from work each day, because we recognized this as a potential fatigue issue." (Hall, Chairman, National Transportation Safety Board 1997)

Hall included with his letter a booklet, "Fatigue Symposium Proceedings," presented November 1–2, 1995, by the NTSB and NASA Ames Research Center. The school bus collision had occurred about a week prior to the symposium. The symposium had many speakers, including leading experts in fatigue.

Secretary of Transportation Frederico Peña indicated that human factors cause about a third of all railroad collisions. He also noted "the insidious danger is that the operator may become dulled enough to miss—or misinterpret—a critical danger signal, or be slow in responding to it."

Dr. Mark Rosekind told the symposium that it is difficult to sleep during the day when you are biologically programmed to be awake, as is the case with swing shift workers who go back and forth between schedules or may revert to daytime schedules on their days off. As you lose sleep, it builds up into a sleep debt, Dr. Rosekind said. (Rosekind 1995)

Dr. David Dinges spoke of the performance effects of fatigue, including slowing reactions by 5 to 25 percent and increasing operator errors, false responding, and memory errors. (Dinges 1995)

Dr. Charles Czeisler said the early morning hours represent a critical zone of vulnerability for individuals in the transportation industry. It was reported years ago that there is a sixteen-fold increase in the risk of a single vehicle truck collision due to sleepiness at that time when compared to the middle of the day, he said.

Czeisler spoke of one telling experiment done in Sweden. Electroencephalogram (EEG) recordings were taken on train engineers on overnight runs. This test measures and records the electrical activity of a person's brain. Additionally, testers were able to determine through eye movements which train engineers were well rested and which were not (EEG and eye movement analyses are different).

In one test, a sleepy train engineer passed a prestop signal and failed to apply his brakes until about twenty seconds later. Suddenly, the engineer's heart rate, a third measurement, jumped just at the point at which he applied his brakes. There was not another stop signal in that twenty second interval, yet it took twenty seconds for the signal to pierce his consciousness and for him to realize that he had seen a stop signal and had not yet applied his brakes. (Czeisler 1995)

Metra commuter service trains have only one person, the engineer, operating the train. Freight rail lines have two people in the front end of the train, the locomotive engineer and the conductor.

Steve Frankowiak, when working as an engineer on the Metra/ UP commuter line, told me he has gone to work tired every day except one. Steve also added that on top of his wish for improving safety would be to add another person in the locomotive cab with some engineering experience or training. Other Metra locomotive engineers have told me how busy they are and how important it is to have another person in the locomotive compartment to help with the operation of the train.

In July 2010, the *Chicago Sun-Times* reported on Metra's excessive overtime payroll. The article indicates that about 11 percent of total payroll expenses went to overtime pay. Metra locomotive engineer and local chairman of the Brotherhood of Locomotive Engineers and Trainmen Charles Lough typically works a six-day, seventy-three-hour workweek, according to the article. He was quoted as saying Metra allows overtime "because it is the cheapest way to go. It's cheaper than hiring two people and paying benefits for two people." (Wisniewski, Fusco and Golab 2010)

Retired Metra/UP locomotive engineer Steve Frankowiak stated that overtime hours are paid at straight time on Metra commuter lines.

Between January 1, 1990, and October 25, 1995, when the Fox River Grove train–school bus collision occurred, Metra trains had been involved in 215 highway/rail crossing incidents, resulting in sixty-two fatalities and ninety-five injured, according to Illinois Commerce Commission statistics. There were systemic problems in the way Metra was operating its trains.

An NTSB pronouncement of operator fatigue as a contributing factor would have been meaningful in improving safety. A stronger argument could have been made to reduce the Metra engineer's work hours, eliminate split shifts, have two-person crews operating each train, and have less driving to and from work.

When I asked Steve Frankowiak, who had thirty-eight years of railroading experience as a brakeman, fireman, and mostly as a locomotive engineer what would be a top priority on his wish list if he could make railroading safer, he stated that adding another person in the locomotive cab would probably be number one. He also indicated that person should have training to qualify as a locomotive engineer.

Some years later, after a horrific head-on collision in Chatsworth, California, Metrolink, the involved commuter rail system, began using two-person crews.

At the time of the collision, Ford Dotson Jr. was a hardworking Metra locomotive engineer who was operating a train on a long split shift and driving an additional hour and twenty minutes, each way, to and from work. Dotson, like other locomotive engineers involved in train collisions, is also a collision victim who has, in all likelihood, spent many years suffering stress trauma caused by this collision.

He spoke at the DuPage Railroad Safety Council 2008 safety conference where he described the collision as "the worst day of my life," according to the Daily Herald. "I automatically put the brake down. I had no idea what the bus was going to do at this time. I also started the whistle warning signal. I was trying to get the bus driver's attention to say, 'I'm here and I can't stop.'"

After the collision, the train had come to a stop about a quarter of a mile past the crossing, and although he wanted to rush out and help, Dotson said he was ordered by the railroad to remain in his train. For the next several days, he was interviewed and also testified before authorities. During that time, he reported that he felt like "I didn't have no soul. It left my body." (Pyke, Solutions to Rail Safety Tricky but Worth It, Experts Say 2008)

Recommendations from the NTSB carry substantial weight for positive change. Almost immediately after the Fox River Grove collision, the NTSB announced that the timing of the Algonquin Road signals was too short. Action to correct similar problems at other crossings in Illinois took place at once. (Jimenez and Brown 1995)

Although fatigue was a factor, I now believe that the active warning devices did not provide the minimum required twenty seconds of warning, and that Engineer Dotson did react, as he had stated, when he saw the bus moving across the tracks, but that he lacked location awareness to realize that his reaction actually occurred when he was about ten seconds from the crossing, and not at the more than twenty seconds from the crossing that he had thought it had.

In a safety recommendation dated June 1, 1999, directed to the US Department of Transportation (DOT) secretary Rodney Slater, NTSB chairman Jim Hall revisits three safety recommendations made ten years earlier for reducing operator fatigue as a contributing factor in transportation collisions. The recommendations were:

1) A coordinated research program on the effects of fatigue,
2) Develop and disseminate educational material for the transportation industry regarding shift work, work and rest schedules, and proper regiments of health, diet, and rest, and
3) Review and upgrade regulations governing hours of service for all transportation modes to assure that they are consistent and they incorporate the results of the latest research on fatigue and sleep issues.

Hall indicated that the NTSB was extremely disappointed with the lack of rule-making by the DOT concerning hours-of-service regulations. "Despite the many statements made by the DOT about the importance of addressing fatigue in transportation, only one of three intermodal recommendations issued to the DOT more than ten years ago has been fully implemented," according to Hall's letter. That recommendation was the coordinated research program on the effects of fatigue.

The difficulty in determining the incidence of fatigue-related accidents is due, at least in part, to the difficulty in identifying fatigue as a casual or contributing factor in accidents," Hall wrote. "There is no comparable chemical test for identifying the presence of fatigue as there is for identifying the presence of drugs or alcohol; hence, it is often difficult to conclude unequivocally that fatigue was a casual or contributing factor in a accident. In most instances, one or more indirect or circumstantial pieces of evidence are used to make a case that fatigue was a factor in the accidents.

This evidence includes witness statements, hours worked and slept in the previous few days, the time the accident occurred, the regularity or irregularity of the operator's schedule, or the operator's admission that he fell asleep or was impaired by fatigue. Despite the difficulty in identifying fatigue as a casual factor, estimates of the number of accidents involving fatigue have been made for different modes of transportation. The estimates vary from very little involvement to as high as about one-third of all accidents. (Hall, Letter to Secretary Rodney Slater, U.S. Department of Transportation 1999)

Chairman Hall's comments support my argument that engineer Ford Dotson Jr. was fatigued. When comparing Mr. Dotson's testimony to the actual on-scene event recorder data, he thought he had reacted much sooner than he actually had. His sleep habits in the five days preceding the collision went from long stretches of sleep on the weekend to weekday split shifts. In addition to long hours spent operating trains during morning and evening rush hours, he also drove a long distance to and from work. The round trip from home to work and back took him about two hours and forty minutes each day. The collision occurred in the early morning—a critical zone of vulnerability for individuals in the transportation industry.

In addition to a single most-likely cause, collisions often have several contributing factors. To change or to eliminate any one contributing factor could make a significant positive difference toward improving safety. At the time of the Fox River Grove train–school bus accident, the crossings in the community were, and still are, "quiet-zone" crossings.

The locomotive engineer operating the train is excused by state law requiring train horns to be sounded and also determines when and if the train horn will sound. On June 1, 1995, about five months before the collision, the US Department of Transportation published a stunning press release that reads in part:

<u>FOR IMMEDIATE RELEASE,</u> Thursday, June 1, 1995

Motorists Suffer 84 Percent More Crashes at Highway-Rail Crossings Where Train Whistles Are Banned, According to FRA Report

In the release, FRA Administrator Jolene M. Molitoris commented "The report clearly shows that train horns significantly reduce the likelihood of highway-rail crashes. Too often, the choice comes down to hearing the whistle of a train or potentially the siren of an ambulance. These horns are saving lives."

The NTSB investigative report did not mention the fact that the crossing was in a "quiet zone." The NTSB seemed oblivious to that fact. The report infers that the train horns started sounding about twenty-three hundred feet, and about twenty-three seconds, from the crossing when, as Engineer Dotson testified, he started the braking process and at the same time started sounding his train horn.

The NTSB performed sound tests from various distances to determine at what level the train horn would have been heard inside the bus where the driver was sitting. The tests at different distances show that they could be heard at fairly high levels, at about seventy-four decibels and above. However, the NTSB concluded that for several reasons, including bus insulation from outside noises and noise in the bus from the radio possibly playing, the bus driver was unable to hear the train horn, or if the driver heard it, she was unable to recognize it as a train horn sound. They seemed to ignore the possibility that the train horn was not first sounded when the NTSB believed it was, at about twenty-three hundred feet from the crossing.

If the train horn first sounded when Dotson actually began the stopping process as Dotson testified, that would have been about ten seconds or less before reaching the crossing. In the final NTSB Accident Report, and other NTSB investigative reports that relate to the Fox River Grove accident, I could not find information as to when the event recorder indicated the train horn sounded.

Testimony given by Fox River Grove Police Chief Paulson, who already had been at the crossing to observe its dangers as part of an independent investigation, stated what he saw and heard that morning. The bus was stopped at the red light and "within seconds the railroad warning lights came on and the gates dropped. The gate on the north side struck the bus and bounced two or three times on the left side of the bus. I heard what sounded like a train horn, possibly two blasts. I look to the west (my right) and saw a light and control cab car. As I exited the vehicle, the train, an express, struck the rear left portion of the bus."

The school bus driver indicated she had never heard the train whistle.

Two days after the collision, student Zach Davis, fifteen, told investigators "The driver looked up as I looked up after hearing the horn. She said, 'Oh,' and I said, 'Oh,' at the same time. I looked into the driver's rearview mirror and saw the train...when I looked up after hearing the horn, the train hit and my head snapped back. I heard glass and metal grinding." (Carpenter and Nicodemus 1996)

The lack of a timely recognition of the approaching train, either by sight or sound, were additional contributing factors.

I still believe that triangular lighting would have made a difference in train recognition by those in the bus, and a less tired engineer may have presented a less confusing timeline of when events occurred.

However, I now believe that the warning signals and gates at the crossing malfunctioned and gave a far shorter warning than twenty seconds, and that the train horn was sounded for a far shorter period than the NTSB report suggests.

A timeline analysis shows a glaring conflict in Mr. Dotson's testimony and the train's event recorder. The NTSB never attempted to explain why. My explanation would be that Mr. Dotson had traveled the same route many times. Warnings at both the Lincoln grade crossing—just northwest of the Algonquin crossing—and the Algonquin crossing normally activate at about the time the train is crossing the bridge. Mr. Dotson, not well rested, had instinctively thought that was when the bus was crossing because the warnings at the crossing had not yet activated.

The chapters that follow detail incident after incident, both at crossings or at switches, in which I believe the most significant contributing factors were malfunctioning signals.

Here are some other facts to support my argument.

The event recorder in the Union Pacific signal bungalow at the crossing was not working on the day of collision. This recorder would have indicated when the signals had been received to activate the crossing warning devices. If not working properly, and there was a delay in signal activation because of a malfunction, one added contributing factor would have been brought to light, and the liability would have somewhat shifted.

It is up to the reader to draw his or her own conclusions, but Pulitzer Prize–winning author Walt Bogdanich does lead one down a path of question. Two paragraphs, although not referring to this specific collision, are worth noting in his well-documented article:

Union Pacific's conduct is a stark example of how some railroads, even as they blame motorists, repeatedly sidestep their own responsibility in grade-crossing fatalities. Their actions range from destroying, mishandling or simply losing evidence to not reporting the crashes properly in the first place, a seven-month investigation by The New York Times has found.

Union Pacific stands out. In one recent 18-month period, seven federal and state courts imposed sanctions on Union Pacific, the nation's biggest railroad, for destroying or failing to preserve evidence in crossing accidents, and an eighth court ordered a case retried. One sanction has been overturned on appeal. (W. Bogdanich, J. Nordberg and T. Torok, et al. 2004)

According to state maintenance records, there had been ten signal complaints since January 1995 at the Algonquin Road/Northwest Highway traffic signal, and at least seven appear to have focused on problems with the synchronization of the stop light and the railroad warning gate. (McKinney, 10 Signal Complaints Tallied in '95 1995)

In testimony before the NTSB, Fox River Grove Police Chief Polston stated that he had observed problems with the timing of the warning signals and traffic lights in the days just prior to the collision and alerted the Illinois Department of Transportation (IDOT). The type of crossing where the accident occurred is known as an *interconnected* crossing. The warnings at the crossing and the traffic signals, when working properly, are linked together and synchronized to ensure safe passage for traffic and pedestrians. He was at the crossing with Bob McWilliams from IDOT that morning and witnessed the collision.

Chief Polston, a seasoned police officer, also testified that he'd heard one or two brief blasts from the train horn just prior to the collision.

The accident history at the Lincoln and Algonquin crossings, both similar crossings and very close to each other, shows just how dangerous these crossings are. Since 1929, when combining the number of collisions from both crossings, there had been about thirty grade crossing accidents (*Daily Herald*, 10/27/1995).

This chapter, covering the Fox River Grove collision, had been written, and I thought—with the exception of some final editing—I had completed it. Over the years, I had cataloged in a series of binders many documents, testimony, and articles that I had acquired. There was a small handful of documents that, for whatever reason, sat uncatalogued in a pile. As I browsed through them, I found a letter I had written to an FRA inspector whom I knew. The letter was dated March 28, 1999, and I had long ago forgotten about it.

In my letter to the FRA inspector, I referenced the Amtrak collision in Bourbonnais, Illinois, that had occurred just weeks earlier, on March 15, 1999, when an Amtrak passenger train had struck a loaded semitrailer. Many died or were injured. The NTSB believed the signal at the crossing was working properly. Witnesses and the Illinois State Police reported otherwise.

My March 28, 1999, letter included the following paragraph: "In fact, what if at both of these major accidents there were timing problems in the warning system that occurred so infrequently that they were not detected after accident inspections? I think what it may indicate is that there may be a serious signaling problem that we may be overlooking."

What has occurred over time is a haunting example of how right I now believe I was.

"To the parents, relatives and friends of those who have been killed or injured in railroad accidents, many of us share your grief and are working toward making all communities safer. We haven't forgotten your friends and loved ones." (Swimmer, Horrible Day 1996)

Jeff Clark, Stephanie Fulham, Susanna Guzman, Michael Hoffman, Joe Kalte, Shawn Robinson, and Tiffany Schneider lost their lives at the Fox River Grove crossing. Many others were injured—both physically and emotionally. Engineer Ford Dotson has also suffered severe emotional trauma.

The City of New Orleans

. . .

Bourbonnais, Illinois, March 15, 1999

Amtrak's City of New Orleans was about fifty-one miles into a trip of 921 miles from Chicago to New Orleans when it collided with a semitrailer carrying forty-six thousand pounds of rebar steel. It was 9:47 p.m. on March 15, 1999, when the collision occurred at the McKnight Road (DOT/AAR 288933B) crossing in Bourbonnais, Illinois. The fiery crash resulted in eleven fatalities, eighty-nine injuries and over fourteen million dollars in property damage. "NTSB Railroad Accident Report PB2002-916301, NTSB/RAR-/01."

City of New Orleans, notice train cars parked on siding obscuring distance to crossing

The Illinois State Police, along with the NTSB, investigated the collision but are in disagreement with the NTSB on the probable most significant contributing factor. Were the active warning devices, flashing lights, bells, and gates working properly? The NTSB says yes; the Illinois State Police say no.

Developing a timeline leading up to the collision is critical. When did the warning signals at the crossing begin activation, and were the devices working properly and continously once activated? When did the truck driver first become aware of a train approaching? When did the locomotive engineer first become aware of the truck in the crossing? When was the train horn sounded, how was it sounded, and was it heard by the truck driver involved in the collision?

The FRA requires a minimum of twenty seconds of activation time of the active warning devices at a crossing prior to the train entering that crossing. In Illinois, at crossings with gates, the gates can take *no longer* than fifteen seconds to reach horizontal once activation begins, meaning the gate must be completely horizontal for a minimum of at least five seconds before a train enters the crossing. Once the warning lights begin flashing, vehicles are required to stop and not enter the crossing.

Railroads often set longer warning activation times, or buffers, into their active warning systems. When signals and gates are working properly, and vehicles stop as required, any vehicle already in the crossing when activation starts would have time to clear that crossing.

The system at McKnight Road was set to activate at twenty-six seconds, meaning if the system was working properly, the gate would have been at a complete horizontal position for about eleven seconds prior to the train's entering the crossing. The railroad had built six seconds of additional buffer time into their active warning system.

If working properly, a moving truck would surely have had to swerve around downed gates to be in the crossing when the train entered the crossing.

John R. Stokes, the truck driver of the truck involved in the collision, stated that the crossing lights started flashing when he was "right on top of the track," and if he stopped suddenly he would have had a problem with his load and possibly stopped on the tracks. So he decided to accelerate his truck and clear the crossing.

His statement of when the flashing lights began is supported by several witnesses. One of the witnesses, Luis Nieves, testified that Mr. Stokes entered the crossing as the lights were flashing and the crossing gate arm struck the semitrailer as it was moving across the tracks.

Another witness, Aubrey O. Fosburgh III, testified that, from his position, he saw neither lights flashing nor the gate lowering. (Karlak, NTSB Hearings Try to Sort Out Fatal Train Crash 1999)

Another witness, an unnamed security guard at a nearby company, saw the warning lights begin to flash about five seconds before the collision.

However, one witness, Troy Schultz, was operating a nearby crane. He was fifty feet up and about sixteen hundred to eighteen hundred feet from the crossing and testified that he saw the warning signals first begin flashing at about twenty seconds before the collision. He lost sight of the flashing signal as he operated his crane to perform a specific task and then saw the collision. The NTSB investigators performed tests of how long it took the crane operator to perform the specific task, and the average time was between twenty-four to twenty-six seconds.

The Illinois State Police, in their investigative report, said Mr. Stokes approached the crossing at fifteen to twenty mph, drove past flashing red lights, but the crossing gates did not descend until he was on the tracks. A warning gate hit the side of the semitrailer. Witnesses, tests at the crossing, and mathematical calculations showed the traffic warning system was not working normally. (Main 2002)

The NTSB's Bourbonnais railroad accident report was accepted by NTSB's Board on February 5, 2002, nearly two years after the collision. In it, they indicated that, based on system tests and physical evidence, the grade crossing signal lights began flashing at least twenty-six seconds before the train's arrival at the McKnight Road grade crossing, and the crossing gates likely lowered as designed. Mr. Stokes had ample time to stop safely, and instead decided to attempt to cross ahead of the train. (Board, PB2002-916301, NTSB/RAR-02/01 Adopted 2002)

In my opinion, another strong argument can be made for the following scenario. All of the eyewitness accounts are essentially correct. The event recorder for the gates at McKnight Road crossing is correct. The system was told to activate twenty-six seconds before the collision, and the red lights at the crossing began flashing at twenty-six seconds before the collision.

However, the red lights at the crossing did not continuously flash, they stopped and began again just prior to Mr. Stokes's entering the crossing. The gate crossing arm had remained up during most of those twenty-six seconds but did begin its downward movement and struck Mr. Stokes's semitrailer as it was moving across the tracks. The warning system at McKnight Road had malfunctioned.

The conflicting eyewitness testimony is only one of the significant factors that supports my belief.

In the NTSB's Bourbonnais accident report under the section titled Grade Crossing Signal Malfunction History is the following:

Two activation failures at the McKnight Road crossing have been reported since the March 15, 1999, collision. On March 29, 1999, [at] about 12:32 a.m., the signal system provided only 6 seconds of warning time before the arrival at the crossing of a northbound IC freight train. Investigation revealed a broken bond wire in a switch south of the crossing that temporarily shortened the length of the approach circuit and delayed detection of the train by the signal warning system. [At] about 11:29 p.m. on April 9, 1999, the gates began to cycle up and down while a southbound IC freight train occupied the crossing. In this instance, soybean meal had leaked from a car in the train and had built up between the train wheels and the rail. The material effectively acted as an intermittent insulator that prevented the signal circuit from detecting the presence of the train. In both instances, the event recorders indicated that the signal [had] system failed to provide the intended warning time.

At the NTSB hearings on this collision held in September 1999, John Sharkey, general manager of communications and signals for the Canadian National /Illinois Central Railroad (IC) testified and gave light to yet one more activation failure when he stated that, in the months since the collision, there had been three activation failures at the crossings when at least twenty seconds of warning time was not given to motorists. (Skertic 1999)

In the year before the Bourbonnais accident, there had been four false activations reported at the McKnight Road crossing. (Bogdanich, Nordberg and Craven McGinty, et al. 2004)

The NTSB's Bourbonnais railroad accident report stated that in 2000, the FRA had 63,243 grade crossings in their crossing inventory with train activated warning devices and that 596 activation failures were recorded nationwide (Board, NTSB PB2002-916301, NTSB/RAR-02/01 Adopted 2002)

The *New York Times* did an analysis of government records from 1999 through 2003 and found that there were at least four hundred grade-crossing accidents in which the signals either did not activate or were alleged to have malfunctioned. At least forty-five people were killed and 130 were injured. The railroads are required to maintain the signals and tracks they own. (Bogdanich, Nordberg and Craven McGinty, et al. 2004)

If the statistics are to be believed, and 1999 somewhat mirrored 2000, then there would be a low probability of even one such activation failure in a year at a specific crossing, let alone three within about a six-month period. Even though the McKnight Road crossing on March 15, 1999, drew the attention of railroad inspectors and investigators from Illinois and national agencies, it continued to have safety problems.

In October 2000, Illinois Governor George Ryan announced plans to spend $3.5 million dollars to improve a crossing near the McKnight Crossing and then close the McKnight Crossing. Governor Ryan, who lived in Kankakee, near the accident site, indicated that crossings in the area have been dangerous for years. He also pointed out that in August 2000, a train narrowly missed striking a steel laden truck at the McKnight Crossing. That incident was eerily similar to the 1999 accident. (Heinzmann 2000)

In 2006, the McKnight Road crossing was closed permanently.

The NTSB places significant importance on data recorders. A Safetrain's Module 80015 data recorder was in place at the crossing at the time of the collision. It indicated that the active warning device system was told to activate twenty-six seconds before the collision. However, it did not show if or when the active warning devices actually did activate. This was testified to by John Sharkey from the IC at the September 1999 hearing. (Skertic 1999)

The NTSB stated that the most likely cause of a single gate not to lower would have been a failure of a motor control relay to open when it was de-energized. Were this to happen, the hold-clear mechanism would remain energized, and the gates would not be released (Board, PB2002-916301, NTSB/RAR-02/01 Adopted 2002)

A later chapter points to a May 11, 2000, FRA-published Notice of Safety Advisory involving Model B1 relays manufactured between the years 1965 and 1985 by General Railway Signal (GRS). On occasion, the faulty relays would not work in a timely manner. This particular model relay may or may not have been part of the warning signal system in place at the McKnight Road crossing, but the safety advisory should have put both investigators and railroads on notice that relays were problematic. It certainly deserved mention in the NTSB accident report if for no other reason than to inform the reader whether this was a model in place at Bourbonnais and to give railroads additional notice of a system with a relay problem.

Warning bells, lights, and gates do from time to time act erratically. One particular incident I personally witnessed was at Main Street in Downers Grove. As I sat in Starbucks viewing the crossing, the warning lights flashed, the gates would go down partway, then completely upright, and then continue repeating this sequence over and over again. Almost immediately cars on busy Main Street began to ignore the malfunctioning crossing warnings and crossed the tracks. This is on the busy, three-track BNSF system that sees about 160 train movements a day.

Prior to the March 15, 1999, Bourbonnais collision, the truck driver, Mr. Stokes, had recorded several moving violations and had previously had his CDL driver's license suspended for not paying a fine. On the evening of March 15, 1999, Mr. Stokes had driven a truck many more hours than he was legally allowed to and had falsified his required logbook. He was tried, and, in 2004, found guilty of these violations and sentenced to two years in prison. He was not found guilty of causing the collision. He died in 2007. (Wikipedia n.d.)

Likewise, the Amtrak locomotive engineer's work history was not unblemished. Per the NTSB accident report:

In testimony at the Safety Board's public hearing, the train engineer, age 52, stated that he had worked as a railroad engineer for almost 25 years before this accident. Records indicate that he was hired by Amtrak on March 18, 1987. According to his testimony, the engineer had operated over the territory in which the accident occurred for 12 years before the accident date, and records showed that his original qualification date over that territory was December 2, 1988. Amtrak terminated the engineer's employment on July 18, 1989, for passing a stop signal. He was reinstated on August 10, 1989. He was again terminated on March 26, 1990, for incurring three rules violations. The violations involved derailing cars, failure to observe and obey speed limit, and violations of operating rules and instructions.

The sounding of a train horn before almost every grade crossing in the United States is mandatory, and such was the case at the McKnight Road crossing. It is to be sounded fifteen to twenty seconds before the crossing in a pattern of two longs blasts, a short blast, and another long blast, and this pattern is to be repeated until the train enters the crossing. The St. George Road grade crossing was about half a mile north of the McKnight Road crossing, and a whistle post was in place about a quarter mile north of the St. George Road crossing, or at 4,000 feet north of the McKnight Road crossing. The train horn should have started sounding at about the time it reached that whistle post, and the pattern sequence should have continued for about thirty-five seconds until the train entered the McKnight Road crossing. A train horn in ideal conditions can be heard 4,000 feet ahead of an approaching train, and the sound level should increase as the train moves closer to the crossing.

The sounding of the train horn is meant to warn those ahead of the approaching train not to enter the crossing, and if already on the crossing to exit immediately. At crossings with active warning devices, it is intended to be a redundant safety feature in that the train crew sounds the horn, and the train activates the warning devices at the crossing.

The NTSB's accident report on Bourbonnais did not indicate if Mr. Stokes heard the train horn, or if so, when. It certainly implied that the only warning he was aware of was the flashing lights at the crossing.

Two eyewitnesses, Aubrey Fosburgh III and Troy Schultz, testified at the NTSB hearing that they never heard the train horn. Another witness, Luis Nieves, said he heard the horn of the approaching train, but he did not say when he first heard it. Was it just a second or so prior to the collision, or was it fifteen to twenty seconds prior? (Karlak, NTSB Hearings Try to Sort Out Fatal Train Crash 1999)

The NTSB report contains the following excerpt: "The tabular data indicate that the train was traveling about 79 miles per hour as it approached the accident crossing and that the train horn was sounded when the train was more than 3,000 feet from the accident crossing and again when it had approached to within about 1,600 feet of the crossing. The timing of these horn soundings is in accordance with the placement of the 3-crossing whistle post located north of the St. George Road crossing."

Both the vision of Mr. Stokes and that of the Amtrak engineer was obscured by railcars in a rail siding (see glossary for definition) next to and west of the main line. At seventy-nine mph, the train was traveling at about 115 feet per second. Additional text from the report includes the following: "At the time of the accident, about 20 freight cars were standing on the Lambert Grain Company side track closest to the main track. The freight car closest to McKnight Road was 376.5 feet north of the centerline of the grade crossing. An approaching southbound train could not be seen until it had cleared this point."

The other mention in the report of the horn sounding was just several seconds before the collision. "The train engineer, who was the only person in the locomotive cab at the time, stated that he saw the truck slowly moving over the crossing, and he sounded the train horn to warn the truck driver."

The NTSB accident report does not address the question as to why the train horn did not provide the truck driver a timely alert. Some thoughts as to why train horns may not be heard at railroad crossings are; vehicles are better soundproofed, drivers have earphones on, there are barriers between the train and the crossing that reduces the effectiveness of the horn. Train horns are meant to offer a fail-safe redundant warning system if for whatever reason the warnings at the crossing do not alert the driver, passengers or pedestrian that a train is coming. However, in several accidents that I investigated the horn was sounded but not heard by those at the crossing.

Katie Ann Lunn

. . .

University Park, April 16, 2010

In Chicago and its suburban area, it is not uncommon for vehicles to be backed up in traffic. When stopped on tracks at crossings, vehicles are usually able to clear the tracks when traffic in front begins to move. At crossings where there are active warning devices, the warning devices are required by law to be activated at least twenty seconds prior to the train's entering the crossing.

Katie Ann Lunn

Katie Ann Lunn, twenty-six, died on April 16, 2010. Ms. Lunn was a dancer, a dance instructor, and a manager. She was employed at the School of Performing Arts in Naperville, Illinois, and at the Joffrey Ballet School in Chicago. On this day, she had spent a good part of her day watching and assisting nearly four dozen of her students perform at the American Dance Awards at Governors State University in the Chicago suburb of University Park, Illinois.

Ms. Lunn was a thoughtful and happy person who loved her students and her work. (P. Biasco 2012)

I have a friend who taught dance with Ms. Lunn. My friend was deeply moved by Ms. Lunn's death and also spoke very highly of her.

The Canadian National Railroad (CN) had a track crew working at the Stuenkel Road (DOT/AAR 289680) crossing in University Park on April 16, 2010. At 9:40 p.m., Ms. Lunn was slowed down on the tracks because of a traffic backup. She was attempting to clear the crossing when her SUV was struck by a northbound Amtrak train number 392 traveling at seventy-eight mph. She died instantly. (Hilkevitch 2012)

One witness, Lauren Brown, who said she was driving ahead of Ms. Lunn stated "The lights and the gate did not work. It was horrible. I did not know the train was there till it was up on me. The gates did not go down, and there were no lights." (Metsch and Tridgell 2010)

Ms. Brown also stated, "There was no way for us to know a train was coming, and at the point [that] the conductor blew his horn when I was on the tracks, it was too late for anyone to change course." (P. Biasco 2012)

The Stuenkel Road crossing is one that requires the train to sound its horn fifteen to twenty seconds prior to reaching the crossing. It is to continue to sound the horn with two long whistles, a short, and another long until it enters the crossing. Many Chicago-area crossings are "quiet-zone" crossings. This one was not.

The train horn sounding is meant to be a redundant safety measure to either keep people and vehicles from crossing the tracks, or, if already on the tracks, to provide an opportunity to exit them. Fifteen seconds is a significant amount of time. Ms. Lunn either did not hear the train horn or was not able to react in time. Witness Brown, who was in a vehicle ahead of Ms. Lunn, gave the impression, by her statement, that she had heard the horn far less than fifteen seconds prior to the collision.

The incident was investigated by the Illinois Commerce Commission's Dennis Mogan, formerly Metra's Director of Safety and Rules. The event recorder on the Amtrak train showed that the train horn was sounded 1,740 feet from the crossing, which provided about fifteen seconds of warning time. The Amtrak train crew did what they were supposed to do.

A final report was issued about two years after the incident. It found that the track-signal crew that had worked on the tracks had violated work-hour limits, and that the crossing warning devices were activated just two seconds before the collision—not the required twenty seconds. Additionally, the CN did not report the accident to federal authorities until the next day, and, by that time, they had corrected the programming error.

The primary contributing cause of the collision was determined to be that the CN railroad track-signal crew took the warning devices out of service without exercising appropriate procedures to either ensure the devices were operating correctly or to warn train traffic that they were not operating, and to therefore require train speed reductions. The required minimum twenty seconds of warning time was not provided.

The Canadian National railroad admitted liability and eventually settled with Ms. Lunn's estate for six million dollars.

Honoring Our Veterans

. . .

MIDLAND, TEXAS, NOVEMBER 15, 2012

THE DAY STARTED WITH SUCH a wonderful display of community spirit but ended so tragically. Thursday, November 15, 2012, was the first of three days of scheduled events that the volunteer group Show of Support, Military Hunt, Inc., in the west Texas town of Midland, had set aside to honor twenty-four veterans, along with their spouses, of the Wars in Iraq and Afghanistan. The events included a parade, banquets, and deer hunting. This was the ninth annual such event. It was a beautiful day for a parade, with temperatures in the 70s, dry roads, and visibility of ten miles. The parade started at about four o'clock in the afternoon and at times consisted of a band, motorcycles, police cars, and two parade floats filled with the wounded war veterans and their spouses. The parade floats comprised the veterans and their spouses sitting on chairs lined up on flatbed semitrailers. (Parade Where Vets Killed Used Route for 3 Years 2012)

Several poor choices had been made by the parade event organizers and the City of Midland. No Midland parade permit was sought by the organizers, and the City had allowed such a nonpermitted parade since 2009. The parade was to cross a very active and accident-prone railroad grade crossing, when a safer route could have been chosen. The Union Pacific Railroad, which owned and controlled freight traffic, was not notified.

At 4:35 p.m., as the parade traveled south, the second of two floats entered the South Garfield Street crossing. The float involved in the collision was moving at about five mph when it entered the crossing and was struck by an eastbound Union Pacific freight train traveling at sixty-two mph. Some of the veterans and their spouses realized that the approaching train was about to strike the float and scrambled to safety. Many were not so fortunate. There were four fatalities and twelve injuries. The fatalities were: Marine Corps CWO Gary Stouffer, army sergeant major Lawrence Boivin, army sergeant Joshua Michael, and army sergeant major William Lubber.

A flatbed truck, pictured, carrying wounded veterans and their families before it was struck by a train in Midland, Texas. Reporter-Telegram/Associated Press

Traffic lights on southbound South Garfield Street at the intersection with West Front Avenue and the incline leading to grade crossing. NTSB

Aerial view of the crash site, with arrows marking the parade and train routes. (Photo courtesy of Google Maps)

Upon hearing of the accident, my thoughts flashed back to the October 25, 1995, Fox River Grove train–school bus collision. There were far too many similarities: an already dangerous crossing made more dangerous, a vehicle with many occupants almost at a stop on the tracks, with a train bearing down on the vehicle (in the Fox River Grove collision, the bus had stopped on the tracks), a driver without adequate training on when it is safe to cross tracks, inadequate warning times, and a final investigative accident report prepared by the NTSB that either minimized or ignored some clear and present dangers.

The South Garfield Street crossing, (DOT/AAR 796331L), had a long history of vehicle-versus-train collisions. The single-track system averages about twenty-three trains a day, and the maximum track speed is seventy mph. From 1979 through 1997, according to FRA records, there had been ten collisions at this crossing. The average daily traffic count on South Garfield Street in the vicinity of the grade crossing was about sixteen thousand vehicles. Running parallel to the tracks are two streets. West Front Street is about eighty feet north of the track, and West Industrial Street is about sixty-seven feet south of the track. There are traffic signals at both intersections. The City of Midland established a quiet zone at the grade crossing in 2007 that eliminated the mandated sounding of locomotive horns. (Board, NTSB Accident Report, NTSB/HAR -13/02, PB2014-100830, Notation 8462A 2013)

Scott Moore, a sales associate for Consolidated Electrical Distribution, which has offices near the intersection of Industrial Avenue and Garfield Street, stated, "The intersection is the worst in Midland. From my office I hear brakes screeching four or five times a day." According to Mariana Valdez, a cashier at Affordable Tools, "By five p.m., there are too many vehicles in the area."

Even though vehicles on the road often slow down to a crawl near the tracks, trains may go up to seventy mph. According to a 2002

Reporter-Telegram report, the UP strengthened its rail system in the Midland area to handle increased train speeds. (J. Biasco 2012)

The Midland collision mirrored the Fox River Grove incident in that seconds and inches made a difference between life and death. One such heroic example was that of Joshua Michael. Sergeant Michael died in the accident after nudging his wife, Daylyn, off the float moments before it was hit by the train. Sergeant Michael had been wounded in Iraq by improvised explosive devices on multiple occasions, and he suffered a brain injury in 2006. (Koppel and Bustillo 2013)

Where mandatory whistle blowing is required at a crossing, the train whistle pattern is a continuous series of two longs, a short, and then another long until the train enters the crossing. The UP's General Code of Operating Rules, summarized from their website, contains the following rule on horn use: Train is approaching public crossings at grade with engine in front. Signal starts not less than fifteen seconds but not more than twenty seconds before reaching the crossing. If movement is forty-five mph or greater, signal starts at or about the crossing sign, but not more than a quarter mile before the crossing if there is no sign. Signal is prolonged or repeated until the engine completely occupies the crossing(s).

At this "quiet-zone" crossing, whistle blowing was at the discretion of the train crew. The train-whistle pattern first began 7.8 seconds before impact.

If it had been a mandatory whistle-blowing crossing, the pattern would have begun not less than fifteen seconds and not more than twenty seconds before reaching the crossing, and would have continued until the engine completely occupied the crossing. There would have been at least 7.2 seconds of additional whistle blowing in a systematic pattern. The first sequence of whistle blowing would have begun before the float entered the crossing. According to the NTSB timeline, the float vehicle was twenty-five feet from entering the track at 13.5 seconds prior to impact. Mandatory whistle blowing, when combined with active warning devices at the crossing, provides a redundant warning that is used to alert those at the crossing that a train is approaching.

The NTSB, in the Midland collision, like in the Fox River Grove collision, discounted the importance of mandatory whistle blowing as a contributing factor and stated the following:

> The City of Midland established a quiet zone around the grade crossing in 2007 restricting the routine sounding of locomotive horns 24 hours a day. Typically, when not in a quiet zone, a train traveling at 62 mph would initiate a horn sequence about 15 seconds (a quarter mile) prior to reaching a grade crossing. The train horn sequence would have been initiated 5 seconds after the activation of the grade crossing lights and bells. Given the ambient noise surrounding the parade, the use of the lead float's train horn (the lead truck had a train horn installed) throughout the parade, indication by the float driver that he had not heard the grade crossing bells on approach to the grade crossing, and the float driver's expectation of safety, it is unlikely that a typical train horn sequence would have been detected, or if so, properly interpreted.
>
> The NTSB concludes that the float driver's expectation of safety, combined with the noise generated by the parade, likely reduced his ability to hear or properly interpret the grade crossing system warning bells and train horn.

Risk managers' know that the sooner someone recognizes a danger, then the sooner they can react, and often inches and seconds can make a big difference.

The following appears on the Union Pacific website and clearly states their position about "quiet zones":

QUIET ZONES
"Union Pacific believes quiet zones compromise the safety of railroad employees, customers, and the general public. While the railroad does not endorse quiet zones, it does comply with provisions outlined in the federal law." (Union Pacific Railroad n.d.)

The UP website also states the following: "A ban on locomotive horns in Florida was ordered removed by the FRA after it was shown that the accident rate doubled during the ban."

It is hard to advocate for mandatory train horns when the NTSB minimizes the effectiveness of whistle blowing as it did in both the Midland, Texas, and the Fox River Grove, Illinois, collisions.

Federal regulations (49 CFR 234.225) require at least twenty seconds of activation time at the grade-crossing warning system when a train approaches. The UP intended to provide an additional five seconds of a buffer, or at least twenty-five seconds of activation time at the grade-crossing warning system.

In January 2012, many months before the November 15, 2012 accident, the UP had become aware that there was a problem with the timing of the active warning devices at the South Garfield Street Crossing. The UP had planned to correct the problem, but, due to an oversight, the plan was not implemented. At the time of the collision, the warning system at the collision crossing activated twenty-one seconds before the arrival of the train, not the minimum twenty-five seconds as the UP had intended.

The NTSB concluded that the grade-crossing warning system had provided twenty seconds of warning as required by federal regulations. The NTSB did not go into a discussion as to whether this was an adequate length of warning time.

As at Fox River Grove, the grade crossing at Midland was congested, accident prone, and made more dangerous over time. Unlike at Fox River Grove, at Midland, the NTSB did not seem to think the twenty-second time to activate the warnings at the crossing was inadequate.

A UP representative testified at the Safety Board's public hearing in January 1996 that "[w]e design our circuits for 25 seconds to give a 5-second buffer...because there are conditions out on the track that make us unable to give an exact warning time. These conditions are beyond our control, and we know that this warning time is going to fluctuate; so we put in a 5-second buffer to this 20 seconds" ("NTSB, PB96-916202").

The NTSB felt so strongly about the twenty-second warning time in their Fox River Grove report that it was mentioned in their final report: "Federal Highway Administration (FHWA) should convene a technical working group that includes representatives of rail crossing safety organizations to review existing standards and guidelines and develop new ones, if appropriate, on grade crossing safety including the following issues: when interconnected signals should be used, minimum clearance green time, the existing 20-second minimum warning time, critical storage distance, use of near side traffic signals, joint highway agency/railroad/transit inspections, and stopping on tracks" (NTSB, PB96-916202).

Signal Problems

. . .

THE NTSB DOES NOT HAVE adequate resources to investigate all railroad collisions or incidents. They investigate a very small percentage of those that occur, and those that are investigated, are considered major incidents. A major incident usually has multiple deaths, injuries, or significant property damage. The NTSB final accident report, which is usually adopted about one year after the incident, is the result of a detailed investigation. The report gives an overview of the collision, lists what investigators believe are the primary contributing factors, and contains safety recommendations. These reports are available to the public and can be found on their website (http://www.ntsb.gov/investigations/AccidentReports/Pages/AccidentReports.aspx).

Final reports and NTSB recommendations carry great weight and often lead to positive change. Newsletter "Safety Task Force, National Safety Board." Brotherhood of Locomotive Engineers and Trainmen, June 3, 2012.

The next five chapters focus on major incidents investigated by the NTSB. According to the NTSB, each incident was caused by the same significant contributing factor: locomotive engineer error. In each, the NTSB found that track-signal aspects were missed or misinterpreted by the locomotive engineer.

Eyewitness testimony, pattern analysis, a review of documents, interviewing of the former director of safety for Metra who held this title at the time of the Metra incidents, and other factors lead me to a different conclusion. That is, the locomotive engineers and conductors read the signal aspects correctly, but the signal aspects gave incorrect indications, or false clears.

The five accidents reviewed in the next five chapters are listed in the following table.

Date	*Description*	*Location*	*Rail Lines*
April 23, 2002	Head-on collision	Placentia, CA	Metrolink and BNSF
June 12, 2002	Head-on collision	Aurora, IL	Metra/BNSF
October 12, 2003	Derailment mile-post 4.7	Chicago, IL	Metra Owned/ Rock Island
September 17, 2005	Derailment mile-post 4.7	Chicago, IL	Metra Owned/ Rock Island
September 12, 2008	Head-on collision	Los Angeles, CA	Metrolink and UP

At first I had thought that signal problems for railroads were extremely rare, but as I started to review documents received from the NTSB under the Freedom of Information Act (FOIA) and other documents I obtained independently, my concerns about the risks from faulty signals grew.

On May 11, 2000, the FRA published a Notice of Safety Advisory involving Model B1 relays manufactured between the years 1965 and 1985 by General Railway Signal (GRS). In the advisory, the FRA indicated that it was compelled to do so because of concerns for the safety of railroad employees and the general public. The faulty relays did not work in a timely manner. In July 1999, the FRA notified various railroad associations of B1 failures that had been reported in the signal system of the Washington Metropolitan Area Transit Authority. After the July 1999 notification, other B1 relay failures were reported to the FRA. The FRA strongly recommended that railroads accelerate the inspection, testing, repairing, or replacing of the B-1 relay. Alstom Signaling, Incorporated, which had acquired GRS, estimated that approximately two million relays are affected worldwide. (Administration, FRA Notice of Safety Advisory 2000-1 2000)

In a December 22, 2000, letter from BNSF Superintendent R. Read Fay to a locomotive engineer, the superintendent explains that a false clear indication that occurred on December 8, 2000, which caused the engineer to put the train into an emergency stop, was due to a *bad relay*. It was fortunate the engineer had heard radio communications and was expecting an approaching train on the same track. Letter included in the investigative NTSB file received under FOIA. (Fay 2000)

Retired locomotive engineer Steve Frankowiak told me of a false clear he once had in Crystal Lake, Illinois. Fortunately, he saw the train in front of him and was able to avoid a collision.

The FRA safety advisory notice, like the regulation requiring triangular locomotive lighting, only made a strong recommendation. It did not make the inspection of the B1 relay an urgent and immediate safety requirement. The only time a recommendation will improve safety is when it is acted upon. Time and time again the FRA has expressed dissatisfaction with the safety culture at certain railroads. Some examples follow.

On June 22, 2009, at 4:58 p.m. (EDT), an inbound Washington Metropolitan Area Transit Authority (WMATA) Metrorail train struck the rear of a stopped inbound Metrorail train. Nine people were killed and fifty-two injured. The NTSB, in their railroad accident report, indicated that one of the probable causes was a failure of the track circuit modules built by GRS/Alstom Signaling Incorporated that caused the automatic train control system to lose detection of the stopped train and thus transmit speed commands to the moving (striking) train.

The NTSB report stated, "WMATA failed to institutionalize and employ system-wide the enhanced track circuit verification test developed following the 2005 Rosslyn near-collisions, and this test procedure, had it been formally implemented, would have been sufficient to identify track circuits that could fail in the manner of those at Rosslyn and Fort Totten." Additionally, the NTSB added "Shortcomings in WMATA's internal communications, in its recognition of hazards, its assessment of risk from those hazards, and its implementation of corrective actions are all evidence of an *ineffective safety culture within the organization*" (emphasis added, "NTSB/RAR-10/02, PB2010-916302").

For railroad safety civil penalty cases closed in 2007, Metra, the Chicago-area commuter rail system, was fined $439,500 by the FRA in what was classified as provable collectible amounts for 375 signal violations. As is often the case, the FRA and Metra reached a negotiated settlement for about one-half the amount of the fines. (Federal Railroad Administration 2008)

Some six years later, Metra's problematic signal issues continued. In 2013, Metra was ordered by the Labor Department's Occupational Safety and Health Administration (OSHA) to pay thirty-eight thousand dollars to a signalman. A Metra signalman, an employee of Metra for twenty-two years, said he did not have enough time during regular hours to complete required signal tests and asked to do the work on overtime. When he filed the safety complaint in August 2011, his hours were changed and his position eliminated. (Wronski, OSHA Tells Metra to Pay Whistle Blower $38,000 2013)

The FRA determined that a Metra practice called "change of assignment" resulted in the falsification of FRA hours of service logs. These logs are required to ensure public safety. The three-year probe was led by the Illinois Executive Inspector General Ricardo Mesa and was prompted by an anonymous complaint of ghost pay rolling at Metra.

Mesa said "change of assignment" was a practice that allowed Metra conductors or locomotive engineers to take a day off, usually Saturdays. But they marked on time sheets that they did work, and their replacements did not show their time worked. The FRA said that it is pursuing civil penalties against Metra and will issue warning letters against individuals involved. Metra disputed the results of the probe, saying it was "wrought with errors and should not have been published." Metra also said the job swapping did not threaten public safety or break employment laws and gave Metra flexibility in scheduling. (Wronski, State Watchdog Faults Metra for Falsifying Work Logs 2014)

As of June 2014, Metra had performed eleven disciplinary investigations of Metra train engineers. Eight of the eleven were safety related. Of those, five cases were for missing or ignoring stop signals, two were for speeding, and one was for hitting a post in a station. In 2013 there were a total of eleven disciplinary investigations, of which four were safety related. In 2012 there were a total of twenty-one disciplinary investigations of which thirteen were safety related. (Pyke, Investigations of Metra Engineers on Rise for 2014 2014)

In October 2014, the FRA announced the findings from a review of Metra and directed Metra to take immediate steps to "enhance its safety culture, which is an area of concern." The review was initiated after three serious incidents, two of which involved engineers allegedly speeding, and a third involving a train that reportedly went through a red stop signal, over a eight-day span between May 27, 2014, and June 3, 2014. One of the reported speeding incidents occurred at a crossover when the train was traveling sixty-one mph, and the speed limit was forty mph; and the other occurred at a curve when the train was traveling at forty-seven mph, and the speed limit was thirty mph. (Wronski, Feds to Conduct Safety Assessment After 'Scary' 2014), (Wronski, Feds Say Metra Safety 'an Area of Concern' 2014)

A May 17, 2005, letter by Daniel C. Smith, the FRA's associate administrator for safety, focuses on signal and gate activation failures at grade crossings. He writes of three specific activation failures that had occurred in the first four-and-a-half months of 2005. Two of the activation failures resulted in fatal collisions—one in New York and one in Florida. A third activation failure occurred in New York when a train used a crossover from one track to another and had only a second or two of warning at the grade crossing. Fortunately, this did not lead to a collision.

"FRA therefore recommends that railroads look at all locations where a diverging route exists within the start circuit of an active warning system...*FRA notes that while the possibility is very real that unknown conditions or inappropriate operating procedures will result in an accident/ incident*, the vast majority of warning system malfunctions (as defined in 49 CFR .234.3), anomalies and operating errors involving grade crossing active warning systems do not result in accidents/incidents."

The letter calls for increased testing and continued vigilance and states in closing, "In this vein, the FRA recommends that railroads assure that all employees are made aware of these events, as well as other grade crossing safety issues, and that the significance of full and proper warning system operation be stressed." Daniel C. Smith, Associate Administrator of Safety, US Department of Transportation, Federal Railroad Administration, "letter to Robert C. VanderClute, Association of American Railroads," May 17, 2005. (Smith 2005)*Emphasis added*

The Chicago Tribune in a lengthy 2015 editorial stated that, "Positive train control (PTC) is a safety system to backstop human error. Using GPS, wireless onboard radio and other components it can detect an imminent crash or derailment and override the actions of the engineer, stopping or slowing the train. In 2008, a Metrolink train and a freight engine collided head-on in Los Angeles, killing 25 people. This prompted Congress to order passenger and freight railroads to install positive train control by the end of 2015...The National Transportation Safety Board says it has investigated *30 accidents since 2004 that could have been prevented by PTC. Those accidents killed 69 people, injured more than 1,200 and caused millions of dollars in property damage."* (Editorial, Congress, slow this train 2015) *Emphasis added*

Pattern analysis; a 2000 FRA safety advisory regarding faulty relays that affected approximately two million relays worldwide; eyewitness testimony from locomotive engineers, conductors, and third parties; and more; points me in a much different direction. I believe that often it was not operator error, instead it was a malfunctioning signal.

Here are several other false-signal-aspect collisions I found via an Internet search:

* *Chicago Tribune*, May 22, 1987: "Rust on a track of the Chicago, South Shore, & South Bend Railroad apparently prevented a signal from working properly last month when a South Shore commuter train struck a freight train that had rolled down a rail siding into the train's path, said a[n] NTSB investigator. The rust apparently acted as an insulator, preventing the electronically operated signal from tripping to red from green when the car blocked the track, investigator James Finan said. The train engineer went through the signal unaware of the freight ahead and was killed in the crash."

* *Los Angeles Times*, November 18, 1989: "A head-on collision between two trains that killed 13 people in southern Italy was probably caused by a signal fault and human error, investigators said Friday. State railway officials said 34 people were injured in Thursday's crash south of Calabria. Two cars hurled off the tracks after the trains collided on a bend. Investigators said an automatic signaling system was out of order and a backup procedure between stations along the line appeared to have failed."

* *The Wall Street Journal*, December 29, 2011: "The July 23 rear-ending of one high speed train by another on a viaduct in

Wenzhow in eastern China killed 40 people, injured 172 and resulted in losses exceeding $30 million, the report said…During a summertime thunderstorm last July, according to Wednesday's report, a trackside piece of signaling equipment called a[n] LKD2-T1 failed after a lightning strike thereby cutting off the electronic channel for messages to pass between trains and the dispatch computers. Back-up procedures were inadequate to stop a bullet train from Beijing bound for the eastern city of Fuzhou and running at 99 kilometers an hour before it slammed into the back of another train bound for the same southeastern city and moving at only 16 kilometers an hour."

In the United States, signals at a highway/rail grade crossing are required by regulation to activate at the minimum requirement of no less than twenty seconds before a train enters the crossing. Most rail lines have set the activation times at twenty-five to thirty seconds to give people ample warning time to clear the tracks before a train enters the crossing. Again, in rail safety, seconds and inches can often make the difference in whether a collision occurs.

Near my office is the Downers Grove Main Street crossing. About three hundred feet west of the crossing is the Forest Avenue Crossing. One morning in July 2012, I noticed BNSF employees doing track work. That afternoon, I was stopped by the downed gates at Main Street for an approaching westbound train. Looking west, I saw that the gates at Forest Avenue, which would normally activate at about the same time as at Main Street, had remained up. The train was getting closer and closer, yet the gates at Forest Avenue remained up and cars continued crossing. The Forest Avenue gates finally went down when the train was about hundred feet east of Main Street, or about five to six seconds before the train reached the Forest Avenue crossing. Five to six seconds was far short of the required time for activation. I notified the ticket agent on duty at the Main Street Station who immediately made a call.

The next train, a Metra train, dropped off a crew member to act as a flagman, and BNSF maintenance men arrived quickly.

In January, 2015 the NTSB issued a safety alert to all U.S. railroads. In it the NTSB indicated the following problems existed:

> Light-emitting diode (LED) railroad signals may mask nearby incandescent signals, preventing incandescent signals from being visible to train crews. Under some conditions, if LED and incandescent signals are installed in proximity to one another, the LED signal may appear brighter or closer, causing train crews to confuse the sequence of the signals as they approach. This effect may be more pronounced the closer the train gets to the signals. Control points with incandescent signals are at increased risk of being masked when they are located near control points with LED signals, particularly at night. Stacking routes may increase the risk of accidents in areas where LED and incandescent signals are in proximity to one another because of possible signal aspect (color) confusion.

In the accident investigation of a train collision between two UP freight trains on September 25, 2014 near Galva, Kansas, an eastbound freight train on a main track collided with a westbound freight train that was entering a siding. The NTSB concluded that the following occurred. The eastbound freight crew read a much brighter green LED signal aspect that was about a mile beyond that of the closer and dimmer red incandescent signal aspect. This green signal aspect was able to mask out the red signal aspect, and in effect caused what seemed to be a green false clear at the red signal aspect. (NTSB Safety Alert SA-038 2015)

In issuing the alert, the NTSB felt it was a U.S. railroad system wide problem. The NTSB does not have the authority to demand that railroads react to an alert.

Placentia, California

. . .

APRIL 23, 2002
NATIONAL TRANSPORTATION SAFETY BOARD, ACCIDENT Report
Abstracts, NTSB/RAR-03/04, PB2003-916304

ACCIDENT NARRATIVE

The crew (engineer and conductor) of commuter train Metrolink
809 reported for duty at 1:30 a.m. on April 23, 2002, in Riverside,
California. The crew was scheduled to make several trips operating
the same equipment but with varying train numbers during their
tour of duty. They left Riverside at 2:55 a.m. on their first trip and
arrived at Irvine sometime after 4:00 a.m. On the second trip, they
departed Irvine at 4:23 a.m. and arrived at Los Angeles at 5:30 a.m.
For their third trip, they departed Los Angeles at 5:45 a.m. and arrived back at Riverside at 7:05 a.m.

Meanwhile, the crew (engineer and conductor) of freight train
BNSF PLACCLO3-22 (hereafter referred to by its operational identification, BNSF 5340) had reported on duty at Hobart Yard (near
Los Angeles) at 2:30 a.m. on April 23. Between 2:30 and 5:30 a.m., the
crew took charge of the assigned locomotives, coupled them to their
train, and set out one defective car. By the time this was complete,

several priority trains were ready for departure from Hobart Yard, and these trains were permitted to leave ahead of BNSF 5340. The conductor said that while he and the engineer waited for the traffic to clear, he took a 1 1/2 hour nap.[1] BNSF 5340 departed Hobart Yard about 7:30 a.m.

Between Hobart Yard and CP Atwood, the BNSF railroad is multiple-track territory with either two or three tracks. Trains may be operated in either direction on any of the tracks. The train dispatcher requests routes, and the traffic control system[2] moves track switches and displays signal aspects[3] to crews who operate their trains on the designated routes. BNSF 5340 changed tracks several times between Hobart Yard and Fullerton Junction as it negotiated the morning train traffic consisting of Metrolink and Amtrak trains.

At 7:32 a.m., the Metrolink crew, now operating their train as Metrolink 809, departed Riverside on their fourth trip of the day, heading for San Juan Capistrano. On this trip, the train was configured with the locomotive on the rear and the cab car on the front.

The engineer was operating the train from a control compartment in the cab car. Approaching CP Atwood westbound, Metrolink

---

1 *General Code of Operating Rules* Rule 1.11.1 allows napping by one of the crewmembers when the train is waiting for departure [footnote number 4 in source document].

2 A *traffic control system* (typically abbreviated TCS) consists of wayside signals, powered switches, and control points. The dispatcher issues commands to the system to route trains on the desired tracks [footnote number 5 in source document].

3 The signal *aspect* refers to the physical appearance of the signal, which usually involves the display of colored lights, either singly or in different combinations. Although specific signal aspects vary not only by railroad, but sometimes across territories within a single railroad system, the names given to various signal aspects (*clear*, *approach*, *stop*, etc.) are generally uniform throughout the railroad industry and require similar responses from train crews [footnote number 6 in source document].

809 received a *diverging clear* signal to leave BNSF tracks and enter the Metrolink Olive Subdivision...Train BNSF 5340 was moving toward CP Atwood from the west. The engineer recalled that as he approached Basta, which is at MP[4] 163.0 (about 7 miles from C.P. Atwood), he received a signal that required him to slow his train to 30 mph, which he did. He said that he then noted that the next signal displayed approach but changed *to clear* [emphasis added] before the train reached it. He then resumed normal operating speed.

The BNSF crewmembers said they were engaged in a conversation about previous employment; they had both worked at the same oil refinery before beginning their railroad careers. The BNSF 5340 conductor said that he called aloud the signal at milepost (MP) 42.31, the signal before the signal at CP Atwood as clear...and that the engineer repeated clear. According to the transcript of an interview that BNSF officials conducted with the conductor and engineer of BNSF 5340, the engineer acknowledged that he heard the conductor call out clear and that he confirmed it. In a Safety Board interview, the engineer said that he did not see the signal. "My conductor called it before we went under it; by the time I looked up, we were past it." Both crewmembers said they approached CP Atwood thinking they were operating on a *clear* signal and that they thus were not required to stop or even slow the train. (According to data from signal system data loggers, the signal at MP 42.31 was displaying *approach* at the time BNSF 5340 passed.)

Both BNSF 5340 crewmembers said that just before the train reached CP Atwood, they realized that signal 4EA (MP 40.71) was showing *stop*.[5] The train was traveling about 49 mph at the time...

---

4 BNSF milepost numbers increase from 0.0 at San Bernardino to 45.5 at Fullerton Junction. From Fullerton Junction, numbers decrease from 165.5 to 143.4 at Harbor Jct. [footnote number 7 in source document].

5 The *approach* signal at MP 42.31 was intended to prepare the freight train crew to stop short of the *stop* signal at CP Atwood [footnote number 8 in source document].

They said they noticed Metrolink train 809 on the same track heading toward them, and the engineer placed the train brakes in emergency. The Metrolink 809 engineer said he was slowing the train preparing to go through a switch at 25 mph when he saw the freight train coming toward his train on the same track. He also placed his train in emergency, left the control compartment, and ran back through the lower level of the car warning passengers to brace themselves.

As the freight train slowed, the conductor jumped clear of the locomotive at approximately 25 to 30 mph. Soon after, the engineer also jumped clear. The train was traveling about 23 mph when it collided head on with the standing Metrolink train about 1,630 feet past signal 4EA.

A security surveillance video camera at a commercial storage facility adjacent to CP Atwood captured a portion of the collision on tape. The tape shows Metrolink 809 coming to a complete stop with the trailing (third) Metrolink passenger car standing in the center of the video camera view. After being stopped for about 12 seconds, Metrolink 809 is propelled backward as BNSF 5340 makes contact. The BNSF 5340 lead locomotive comes to rest in the center of the video image after both trains have stopped. Based on the known length of the Metrolink passenger cars and of BNSF locomotive 5340, the easterly movement of Metrolink 809 during impact was calculated to be about 243 feet.

SIGNAL SYSTEM

On April 23, 2002, investigators from the BNSF, Metrolink, Amtrak, the FRA, the Brotherhood of Railroad Signalmen, the California Public Utilities Commission, and the Safety Board began a field inspection of the railroad signal system. The post-accident inspection found all signal units, switches, and the signal cases at the intermediate signals and at CP Atwood locked and secured with no indications of tampering or vandalism.

All relay positions were found to be in accordance with the physical location of the accident trains and with the displayed signal aspects. Ground tests were performed, signal searchlight mechanisms were inspected, and lamp operating voltages were verified. Movements of the spectacle arm[6] were smooth with no binding. All mechanisms were found to be operating properly with no exceptions noted. Track connections and insulated joints were inspected, and no exceptions were noted. Information developed from signal system data loggers and dispatch center records during the investigation indicated that this signal at MP 42.31 was displaying *approach* at the time BNSF 5340 passed the signal.

ACCIDENT DISCUSSION

At the time of the accident, that portion of the BNSF signal system governing eastbound trains, such as BNSF 5340, on track No. 2 approaching CP Atwood involved three signals. All three signals were capable of displaying clear, approach, or stop, and the signals changed automatically, depending on train traffic in the vicinity of the control point.

At the time of the accident, the signal governing eastbound movement at CP Atwood, signal 4EA at MP 40.71, was showing *stop* because of the presence of Metrolink 809. Information developed from signal system data loggers and dispatch center records during the investigation indicated that the signal in advance of signal 4EA, the signal at MP 42.31, was displaying *approach* and that

---

6 A *spectacle arm* holds different color lenses that it positions in front of a single lamp to display the proper signal color [footnote number 30 in source document].

the next signal to the west of this signal, at MP 44.03, was display-ing *clear*. As BNSF 5340 proceeded toward CP Atwood, the first signal it encountered was the *clear* signal at MP 44.03. This signal required no special action on the part of the crew, and the train continued at track speed. The next signal was the *approach* signal at MP 42.31. Encountering this signal, the crew of BNSF 5340 should have slowed their train's speed to 30 mph or less and been prepared to stop at the next signal.

But when train BNSF 5340 approached the *approach* signal at MP 42.31, the crewmembers were engaged in a conversation, and the engineer said he was not watching the signal. The conductor called the signal, incorrectly, as *clear*. Although the engineer told BNSF investigators that he confirmed the conductor's call out of the signal as clear, he indicated to Safety Board investigators that he did not, as required by BNSF operating rules, personally observe the signal and identify its aspect. He stated that when he did look toward the signal, his train had already passed it. In this case, the engineer took the word of the conductor that the signal was *clear* and continued to operate the train accordingly. The Safety Board therefore concludes that the BNSF 5340 train crew were insufficiently attentive to the operation of their train, with the result that they failed to see, iden-tify, and respond appropriately to the *approach* signal indication at MP 42.31. By the time the engineer and conductor saw that the next signal, signal 4EA, was displaying *stop* and the engineer placed the train brakes in emergency, the train was traveling too fast (about 49 mph) to be brought to a stop before striking Metrolink 809. Ample distance existed between the *approach* and *stop* signals to allow the train to slow sufficiently to stop short of the *stop* signal and avoid the collision if the engineer had begun braking as required. The Safety Board therefore concludes that had the BNSF 5340 crew operated their train in accordance with the signal indications, the accident would not have occurred.

PROBABLE CAUSE

The National Transportation Safety Board determines that the probable cause of the April 23, 2002, collision of a Burlington Northern Santa Fe freight train and a Metrolink commuter train in Placentia, California, was the freight train crew's inattentiveness to the signal system and their failure to observe, recognize, and act on the *approach* signal at milepost 42.31. Contributing to the accident was the absence of a positive train control system that would have automatically stopped the freight train short of the *stop* signal and thus prevented the collision.

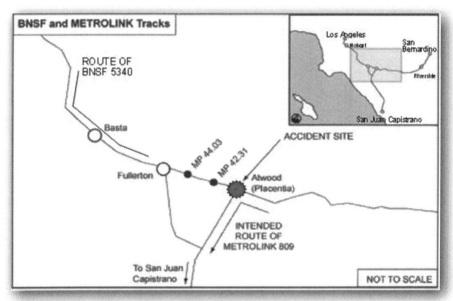

Accident location

Location	Name	Aspect	Indication	Displayed to
MP 44.03	*Clear*	Green	Proceed	BNSF 5340
MP 42.31	*Approach*	Yellow	Reduce to 30 MPH prepared to stop at next signal	BNSF 5340
CP Atwood (eastbound)	*Stop*	Red	Stop	BNSF 5340
CP Atwood (westbound)	*Diverging Clear*	Red over Green	Proceed on diverging route at prescribed speed	Metrolink 809

BNSF track no. 2 signals displayed at time of accident

Aerial photo of accident scene (courtesy of Orange County Sheriff's Department)

Head-On Collision

. . .

Aurora, Illinois, June 12, 2002

Wednesday, June 12, 2002, started out like almost any other workday for Duane Wozek. He had started working for the then-Burlington Northern Railroad in 1972, almost 30 years earlier, and in June 1976 was promoted to locomotive engineer. Wozek's typical workday involved waking up between 4:30 and 4:40 a.m. and reporting to work at about 5:20 a.m. to run commuter trains between Aurora's Transportation Center and Chicago's Union Station until the evening. (NTSB accident report DCA-02-FR-009, interviews, investigative documents 2002)

His thirty-seven-mile runs included many stops at busy suburban commuter stations during the height of the Chicago morning and evening rush hour periods. He had a rest period of about four hours and fifteen minutes between his first morning run to Chicago and his next trip outbound to Aurora, but he did not sleep and, depending on the weather conditions, would either walk or read.

Mr. Wozek would go off duty at 6:44 p.m. Thirteen-plus hours is a long day for anyone, especially for someone doing very stressful work. Running a commuter train on the congested BNSF three-track system during rush hour requires continuous full-minded concentration and quick split-second reaction times. Engineers on any one of Metra's eleven commuter lines will tell you of almost daily near-misses. Sadly, too many locomotive engineers that operate Metra's trains have been involved in incidents involving fatalities. This difficult and stressful work demands quick reactions from well-rested locomotive engineers.

Then add to the mix known negative human factors that take place in stressful jobs, such as elevated blood pressure and disturbed sleep, and the task of operating a commuter train during rush hour becomes even more challenging.

This day would turn out to be a difficult day for many. At 3:20 p.m., Mr. Wozek departed the Aurora Transportation Center heading inbound, or eastbound, to Chicago's Union Station. He sat in the control cab car as his eastbound train was being pushed by a locomotive. His train traveled 1,203 feet and then collided with a westbound Metra commuter train, which had just come to a complete emergency stop. The results were forty-seven injured and the derailment of a locomotive and eight other passenger cars.

After the investigation, the NTSB determined that the probable cause of the collision "was the failure of the engineer and the conductor of [the] train...to comply with the stop signal at the Aurora Transportation Center Station."

A locomotive engineer is instructed by a series of signal aspects. These signals are located at different distances along the tracks and instruct the engineer on what speed the train is to operate, and on train operation as it relates to track placement.

In all the five incidents referenced in the table (see chapter "Signal Problems"), the NTSB reached the same conclusion; the most significant contributing factor in each incident was the failure of the locomotive engineer to correctly read the track-signal aspects.

However, I *disagree* with the NTSB regarding the primary cause and will argue that the track-signal aspects in all five of the major commuter railroad accidents (see chapter "Signal Problems"), in all probability gave an incorrect "false proceed" or "false clear" signal aspect.

Duane Wozek, the locomotive engineer, with almost thirty years of experience, testified the signal aspect read clear, or proceed, when he started to move forward. The train's conductor, Kenny McElroy, with almost twenty-six years of experience, confirmed the signal aspect as clear. BNSF operating rules required that the conductor verify the signal aspect before the train could proceed. An-off duty conductor, Robert Daurer, who had been a conductor for over thirty-six years and who was riding in the lead control cab car as a passenger returning to Chicago for another run, also stated that he saw the signal aspect as clear.

Testing of the signal by the NTSB after the collision would not confirm the signal was clear.

The westbound train number 1235, due at 3:23 p.m., had not yet arrived at the station and was on the same track as Wozek's train number 1270. On this day, track maintenance was being conducted on the track that the westbound train normally would have used. The westbound train crossed over to another track to enter the station and finally stop at a different platform.

Physical evidence showed that a crossover switch was set against Wozek's eastbound train number 1270. Instead of stopping before the crossover, the train violated this crossover switch and continued down the tracks without noticing the violation. The eastbound train went through the switch without derailing, and Mr. Wozek was not aware of the violation.

Wozek testified that in the critical moments of initial train movement, he had focused some of his attention on a door in his compartment that opened to the passenger area. He did not observe that there was a train approaching on the same track and testified that "leaving on a clear indication, I had no reason to believe or think that we would be on the same tracks" and did not notice the crossover was set against him. Only when the engineer on the approaching train shouted, "Stop your train," on the radio did he notice a problem.

"According to the event recorder on train 20, the train continued 664 feet past the crossover switch and attained a speed of 27.5 miles per hour before the train began to reduce speed," according to the NTSB report. "The engineer said that he made an emergency brake application when he heard '[S]top your train,' over his radio. The event recorder could not confirm an emergency brake application because the engineer may also have lifted his foot off the 'dead-man' pedal when he turned to close the cab compartment door, which would have resulted in a penalty brake application." (NTSB accident report DCA-02-FR-009, interviews, investigative documents 2002)

Mr. Wozek testified at a June 2002 hearing led by NTSB Investigator-in-Charge Cyril Gura. The team of questioners included Gregory Smith of the Brotherhood of Locomotive Engineers; and trainmen John Quilty, of the BNSF, Dennis Mogan, of Metra, and Michael Smith, with the FRA.

Mr. Wozek was the only person in the control cab car operating the train. There was no one working with him that could have alerted him of a crossover switch set against his train. When asked if another person in the control cab car would have helped him operate the train, Wozek stated, "it may have." When asked why, he said, "both sets of eyes is always better than one, and I believe several years back the NTSB came out with an article or statement saying that the best safety device any train could have would be two people in the cab." (Wozek 2002)

The locomotive engineer of the outbound westbound train, number 1235, was William Wareham. Wareham had over thirty-four years of experience, including at least five years as a fireman. He had worked in both the freight and commuter services as a locomotive engineer. His immediate response to the collision was both remarkable and heroic. With a moving train coming straight at him, he stayed in his locomotive, operating his train to an emergency stop and warning the approaching locomotive engineer by radioing to him to "Stop your train." Everyone aboard the two trains owes a debt of gratitude to William Wareham.

There is no way to determine why Wareham made such remarkably correct decisions instantaneously. There probably are many reasons, such as his work experience, his character, and possibly his work schedule, which more closely resembled a regular workday than the long split-shift days most Metra locomotive engineers work. He started at 6:03 a.m., had about ninety minutes for lunch, and was off at 3:48 p.m.

Wareham, like other Metra engineers, was alone in his locomotive compartment operating his train. He was asked at the NTSB hearing whether another person in the locomotive or control cab car would help in the operation of the train and testified;

And I think that we all think there should be two engineers on these suburban trains. You are dealing with a lot of people, you know, a lot of, you have an eight-, nine-, ten-car train, you have a thousand, over a thousand people behind you and that is, I know it comes down to a cost factor. I know, we all know that. That is what it basically comes down [to], with another wage you have to pay. But, it comes down to pennies when you take all the people that are running your train, look what could have happened here.

I mean, this is why I am so upset...We are not, we are just speculating right now, *but who knows what another set of eyes might have seen.* We don't know that, but, I am just saying, this should be taken into account. There were reasons why they had firemen on the suburban trains, you know, that was a must-fill job. It was always two engineers, basically it is two engineers out there. I know what it is like to be up there and have two guys up there and it is, it is just a situation that I want to convey. *(Emphasis added)*

Given the testimony of two locomotive engineers on how important it is to have a second person in the locomotive compartment, one might think the NTSB would at least make mention of it in its final report. After all, the NTSB has long recognized the importance of redundancy. There isn't a single mention of that testimony in the NTSB's final "Railroad accident Brief"—not a word. "NTSB, DCA-02-FR-009."

Not included in the final report, it was buried in the testimony of the two locomotive engineers, both of whom knew firsthand that this collision might very well have been avoided had another set of eyes been present—another person who was able to warn, stop, or help operate the train, sitting in the locomotive or control-cab car compartment.

Derailment at
Milepost 4.7 #1

. . .

Sunday, October 12, 2003

The first of two milepost-4.7 derailments

As a low-seniority employee, locomotive engineer Mr. Lonell Toussaint was required to work on several different Metra rail lines, or districts, as they are called within the eleven-line system. Engineer Toussaint had been qualified on Southwest, Rock Island, and Milwaukee Metra lines or districts. With less than three months as a certified locomotive engineer, he had worked in all three of these districts. Each of Metra's districts is unique. There are variations in locomotive equipment, in operating rules, signaling systems, and type of rail traffic. For example, one line might be heavy with freight traffic while another might not, and even the side of the tracks that in-bound and out-bound trains run on could be different. (Board, DCA04MR001 2002)

Metra's crew management department assigns engineers where they are needed and qualified to operate based on seniority. Locomotive engineers with *lowest* seniority are required to operate trains on lines where needed. Although qualified on that line, they often lack meaningful operating experience. One analogy might be comparing an inexperienced teenage driver with a valid driver's license to an experienced adult who has been driving, in all types of traffic, in all types of weather, and with a long history of good driving.

David Daruszka, Metra's assistant supervisor of locomotive engineers responsible for engineer certification and training, testified, "I think one of the problems that we confront with Metra is that people who get forced to get qualified on other districts are the youngest people and usually the least experienced people. They probably don't have the skill set yet to deal with that sort of having all this stuff thrown at them, especially if they're getting bounced around from district to district. It can be very confusing. Overwhelming, in fact." He also stated, "[A] minimum to get familiar with the district and all the jobs on a district, six months."

Metra locomotive engineers are most often alone in the locomotive or control cab car operating the movement of their train. There is no other person in the locomotive compartment or control cab car to help operate the train. Such was the case on October 12, 2003, at 4:38 p.m., when Metra commuter train No. 519 derailed its two locomotives and five passenger cars in the vicinity of the Forty-Eighth Street (milepost 4.7) on Chicago's South Side. The train had departed from the LaSalle Street Station in Chicago (milepost 0.0) at four-thirty in the afternoon. It was carrying a three-man train crew, approximately 375 passengers, and was westbound on Metra's Rock Island Line from Chicago to Joliet when it attempted to cross over from main track one to main track two. The maximum authorized speed for this crossover movement is ten mph. The train derailed at a recorded speed of sixty-seven mph.

There were fifty-four injuries and no fatalities. Damages to the track and equipment exceeded five million dollars. At the time of the collision, recorded weather conditions for Chicago, IL were 68°F, with a visibility of 10 miles.

NTSB/RAR-05/03, PB2005-916303 National Transportation Safety Board, Notation 7615A

The NTSB stated the probable cause was the locomotive engineer's "loss of situational awareness" minutes before the derailment. He had been preoccupied with certain aspects of the train's operation that led to his failure to observe and comply with signal indications. Contributing to the collision was lack of a positive train control system at the collision location. It was alleged that he misread a series of two signal aspects as clear when in fact they were not.

The derailment took place at the crossover at milepost 4.7, meaning it was located 4.7 miles from the LaSalle Street Station. On a straight stretch of track without obstructions, track signals can be seen for long distances. After the collision, NTSB investigators rode on the same stretch of track at about the same time of day and noted that good signal visibility allowed them to see two to three signal aspects in front of the train. The first indication of the upcoming crossover came at milepost 3.9.

The NTSB indicated that it read "proceed prepared to advance on diverging route at the next signal." This was the first indication that the train would need to slow down to cross from track one to track two at milepost 4.7, or four-fifths of a mile down the track.

The first signal should have been visible to the engineer, when traveling at about sixty-eight mph, for about a minute. Engineer Toussaint testified that this signal indicated clear, and that he in fact increased his speed at about milepost 3.9 from forty-eight mph to sixty-eight mph as he approached the crossover at milepost 4.7. The NTSB indicated that the next signal at milepost 4.7 had an indication of diverging clear, which at this crossover meant to slow the train down to ten mph. This signal also would have been visible at about a mile from the crossover or for about one minute. Engineer Toussaint testified that this signal aspect also indicated "clear." The timeline seems to reflect that Engineer Toussaint had about two minutes in total to see a series of two signals and react as instructed.

He not only testified *that he did see* both signal aspects as reading "clear" but affirms that by his actions of increasing his speed from about forty-eight mph at milepost 3.9 to about sixty-eight mph, which is where it should have been at with a "clear" signal.

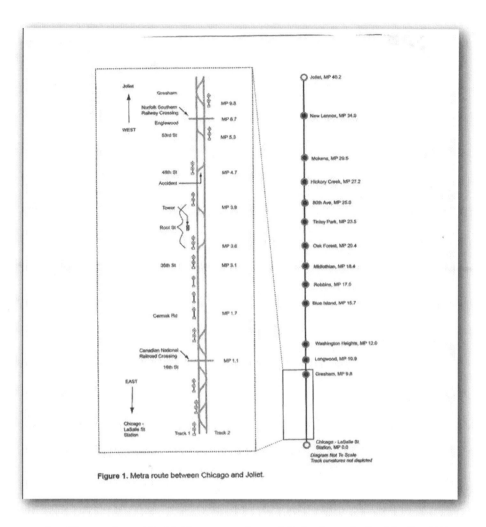

Figure 1. Metra route between Chicago and Joliet.

On December 17, 2003, a panel established on behalf of NTSB interviewed David Rodriquez, senior manager of train operations for Metra. During its investigation, the NTSB had asked Metra's signal department to provide them with a list of signal trouble reports that had been reported by train crews and other railroad personnel.

Mr. Ruben Ryan, the NTSB signal group chairman, started the questioning of Mr. Rodriquez by indicating that the NTSB had requested signal trouble reports from Metra and hadn't received these

records. Mr. Rodriquez indicated that when there is a signal problem, it is noted on a daily Unusual Occurrence Log and the signal
is then repaired by a maintainer. If not repaired that day, it would
then be transferred to the next day's log. At that point there was no
systematic gathering and analysis of signal problems. The report just
stayed with the daily log for the day that it was reported on and was
not accumulated in a database. Mr. Rodriguez could not tell how
many signal malfunctions had occurred over an extended period of
time, where the malfunction occurred, or the type of malfunction
unless he went through the tedious process of reviewing each ar-
chived Unusual Occurrence Log, which he had not done. He testified that on November 11, 2003, he first started to accumulate this
type of information for future analysis on a report called the Signal
Appliance Malfunction (SAM) report. He testified, "[A]ll it is, is the
same information, but now it's just a way to—it's all in one place instead of scattered over different documents."

The gathering and analysis of data is critically important in determining where trouble spots exist, what common problems exist,
and how frequently they occur. David Rodriguez in his testimony
still didn't seem to grasp the value of analyzing the information reported as signal malfunctions.

NTSB has the authority to require signal malfunction information for prior years. Analysis of the data would have helped ascertain
whether these problems were prevalent, whether proper corrective actions had been taken, and whether certain areas were more
troublesome than others. Metra made little effort to determine the
extent of signal malfunctions throughout the Metra system, even
though on June 12, 2002, there had been a head-on collision with
Metra trains in Aurora, which occurred on the Metra/BNSF line.

As I read the testimony given by witnesses at NTSB collision
hearings, I had mixed emotions. The investigations were not truly

independent investigations by the NTSB in that they use what it calls the "party system" (see glossary). Some of these non-independent investigators were employees of the railroad involved in the accident or the union representing personnel involved in in the accident. On the panel questioning Mr. Rodriquez were representatives of the NTSB, the FRA, the Brotherhood of Locomotive Engineers, and Metra. If not outright influencing the course of the investigation, they certainly gave the appearance of a lack of independence.

The NTSB's investigative conclusion was that Engineer Toussaint had lost situational awareness. He lost his locomotive engineer's certification.

The October 12, 2003, collision investigation seemed to focus on Mr. Toussaint's lack of experience; his being preoccupied doing safety checks and reading schedules and orders just prior to the collision; and his working different districts or routes over a relatively short period of time.

The facts also present one additional strong argument why commuter trains should be operated with two people in the locomotive compartment. Although these factors are relevant, Mr. Toussaint, in my opinion, operated his train as instructed by track-signal aspects.

On the day of the collision, Engineer Toussaint started his workday at 1:50 p.m. in Joliet, Illinois, and felt that he was well rested. His trip from Joliet departed at 2:24 p.m. He arrived at the LaSalle Street Station a few minutes before his 3:45 p.m. scheduled arrival time. He did pass some track workers on his trip into Chicago.

He left Chicago's LaSalle Street Station at 4:30 p.m. on his return trip to Joliet. He was using a much different locomotive than the type he had used on the Milwaukee District where he had gained the majority of his experience. In general, the Milwaukee District had older locomotives. The newer locomotives are longer and heavier than the older ones. The engineer's controls are positioned differently, and the locomotives have greater horsepower. On this Sunday, he was operating a multiple-unit train with two connected newer locomotives on the Rock Island District. Mr. Toussaint believed that this was the first time he had ever operated a multiple-unit train with two new engines. The train was accelerating quicker than the trains he had previously operated, and he was checking his speed frequently.

After leaving the LaSalle Street Station at 4:30 p.m. to begin his return trip to Joliet, he was performing required safety checks, and he was also checking his track warrant and track bulletin because he had thought that he should have crossed over from track one to track two at Sixteenth Street and hadn't. He also indicated he had checked his train schedule to see what time he would arrive at the Gresham Station, his first stop. Some, if not all, of these various checking procedures could have been done before the train left the station.

There was a lot going on in the eight minutes or so from when he started his run until the collision. He seemed preoccupied with safety checks, and so forth at a critical time when his attention should have been focused on the track in front of him. In his testimony, Mr. Toussaint seems to indicate that he may have been in over his head. He testified:

> But as an engineer, when you're jumping from district to district, there's a certain amount of confidence that an engineer has to have as far as where he may be on whatever district.
>
> Basically, basics aren't good enough. So when you're out there and you're running an engine, you're running on basics and the basics aren't good enough. Because you have what you call situations. And you have to know how to apply those situations when they come about.
>
> And basically, for the basics, I believed I was qualified as far as for basics. The basic standard operation of rules, basic standard operation of what to do out on the track.

For situations, no, I don't believe I was qualified. The things of that nature takes months, takes experience, you know. And that only comes with time.

For me to say that, you know, what has happened on the Rock could have been prevented with experience, maybe. I'm not sure. But I know what I saw.

In the June 12, 2002, Aurora head-on collision, described earlier, Locomotive Engineer Wozek was alleged to have misread a stop signal aspect and went against a crossover meant for an oncoming train. He, too, seemed preoccupied with safety checks, and so forth at a critical time when his attention should have been focused on the track in front of him. In that collision, the two locomotive engineers involved had combined railroad on-the-job experience of about sixty years, and they both testified that they felt another person to help in the locomotive or control cab car was important.

More of supervisor of training engineers Mr. Daruszka's testimony follows:

Q: Have there been complaints from engineers in the training program when they became certified of this moving around to different districts for training?
Engineer Daruszka: Constantly.
Q: Do you see this as a safety issue?
Engineer Daruszka: Definitely, most definitely.

Daruszka also testified, "If you've been in suburban service long enough, done the same thing over and over and over again, you become very complacent. I certainly can attest to that myself. It's easy to get distracted. You know, you do the same thing, the routine, day in and day out. You've got the same signals, same places every day. It's easy to miss things. They get distracted as well."

Metra trains are often loaded with people, traveling through highly congested areas at up to seventy mph and are involved in far too many collisions. Whether it is lack of knowledge or they believe the costs outweigh the benefits, neither Metra or the NTSB has accepted the importance of operator redundancy in a passenger rail safety.

Derailment at Milepost 4.7 #2

. . .

SEPTEMBER 17, 2005

THE SECOND OF TWO MILEPOST-4.7 DERAILMENTS
IN 2010, I REQUESTED PERMISSION to address Metra's Board of Directors about safety concerns. Carole Doris was the chair of the board at the time. Although I had never met Chair Doris, she knew me as a strong and vocal advocate for railroad safety and a critic of some of Metra's practices. Shortly after my request was made, I received a call from her office indicating that I would be allowed to address the Metra board. It was an act of courage for her to let me speak at the board meeting.

An overview of my testimony along with my written comments for the record can be found in the November 2010 board meeting minutes on the Metra website (http://metrarail.com/content/dam/metra/documents/Board_Information/November%20Minutes2010.pdf).

In preparing for my presentation, I visited the NTSB website and found three major Metra accidents investigated by the NTSB that had occurred after the October 1995 Fox River Grove train–school bus collision. Locomotive engineer error was listed as the major contributing factor for each. In my presentation, I spoke very briefly of the three accidents, 1) the head-on collision in Aurora, 2) a derailment at milepost 4.7, and 3) another derailment at milepost 4.7, from a safety standpoint. At the time, I had not yet reviewed the detailed documentation that had led the NTSB to reach its conclusions.

This book has been a long time coming, and when I finally started writing it, I decided I wanted more information about those three major accidents. I contacted the NTSB for information and eventually received a computer disc with a number of files relating to each of the three incidents. The disc contained testimony from the involved parties and experts, pictures, test results, injury reports, and discipline reports. I found the information both interesting and revealing. In each of the accidents—the June 12, 2002, head-on collision in Aurora, the Chicago derailment of October 12, 2003, and the derailment of September 17, 2005—the NTSB determined that the locomotive engineers had missed or misread track-signal aspects.

A fourth major commuter train collision occurred in Los Angeles, on September 12, 2008. This collision, known as the Chatsworth collision, claimed twenty-five lives, with over one hundred injured. The NTSB again indicated the probable cause as engineer error on the part of the locomotive engineer on the Southern California Regional Rail Authority (Metrolink) commuter train, as he allegedly missed or misread signal aspect.

And finally, after I thought the book was nearly finished, I came across a fifth major commuter train collision, a head-on collision in Placentia, California, on April 23, 2002. The NTSB also alleged operator error of a missed or misread signal aspect.

There is a common factor in all five incidents. They occurred on tracks near where a train would cross from one track to another.

This chapter tells of the Metra September 17, 2005, derailment. The following chapter tells of the Chatsworth September 12, 2008, collision.

The locomotive engineers in the five major commuter railroad incidents—three head-on collisions and two derailments—as well as three on-duty conductors and an off-duty conductor, and three independent eye witnesses may very well have read the signals correctly, and the signal aspects in all the incidents read clear. The probability of the locomotive engineers operating their trains as directed by track-signal aspects is considerably greater than that of the engineers missing or incorrectly reading the track-signal aspects. There may very well have been signal anomalies that could not be duplicated in NTSB testing results.

Michael Rene Smith was an experienced locomotive engineer. Prior to joining Metra in 2005, he had been both a conductor and a freight train engineer for CSX Transportation (CSXT). He had worked at CSXT since October 10, 1998. During his last three years at CSXT he was operationally tested by his supervisors 110 times, which resulted in twelve recorded failures. He also had several field administrative sessions with his CSXT supervisor, the most recent, on March 20, 2005, for using an unauthorized radio and quarreling with a conductor while on duty and on company property. Metra indicated that it was not aware of his problems at CSXT—only that he was certified as a locomotive engineer.

At CSXT, unlike at Metra, there are two people in the locomotive compartment operating the train: an engineer and a conductor. At CSXT, the calling out to each other of track-signal aspects is required, with each signal aspect called and acknowledged by the other person in the locomotive, either the engineer or the conductor. The engineer also is required to call out the signal aspect on the train's radio. Mr. Smith knew how critically important the correct reading of track-signal aspects were when he was employed at Metra; his employment at CSXT taught him that.

Mr. Smith entered Metra's accelerated training program and became certified as a locomotive engineer on August 30, 2005. The morning of Saturday, September 17, 2005, was sunny and warm with the temperature hovering in the mid-sixties. It was what Smith later described as "pretty much a standard morning." At about seven o'clock, the train crew, consisting of Mr. Smith, a conductor, an assistant conductor, and a collector, reported for work in Joliet, IL. The crew held a job briefing before beginning their 7:24 a.m. run to Chicago's LaSalle Street Station. At 8:35 a.m., the train was involved in an accident that claimed two lives, injured 129 people, and caused $6.35 million in damage.

A crossover switch requires the train to cross from one track to another, and was again a contributing factor in this collision, as in the four other major incidents investigated by the NTSB and referred to in the beginning of this chapter. And, once again, the NTSB identified the probable cause as being the engineer's failure to operate the train in accordance with signal indications.

Mr. Smith stated he observed all clear signals, allowing him to accelerate his speed from forty mph to seventy mph as he approached the crossover at milepost 4.7 at Forty-Seventh Street. As the train reached the top speed, he looked down and noticed the switch was lined up for a diverging route, meaning it was to leave track two and traverse to track one. In order to safely take the crossover, the speed of the train should have been ten mph at this point.

In fact, if the signals had indicated a crossover was approaching, his first signal-aspect indication would have been at Fifty-Third Street where the signal aspect would have shown **"approach diverging."** He would have seen this signal about two minutes before the milepost 4.7 crossover. There would have been another signal at Forty-Eighth Street, which would have shown **"diverging clear."** The two signals would have given Mr. Smith ample time to slow down his train. When asked what steps he would have taken if he had been given those signal aspects, Smith answered, "If I would have had those aspects, I would have had to reduce speed to the ten-mile-an-hour speed through the crossover."

Mr. Smith was emphatic when he testified "Well, Fifty-Eighth Street, I also observed a **clear.** Fifty-Third Street a **clear.** Forty-Seventh a **clear**" (emphasis added).

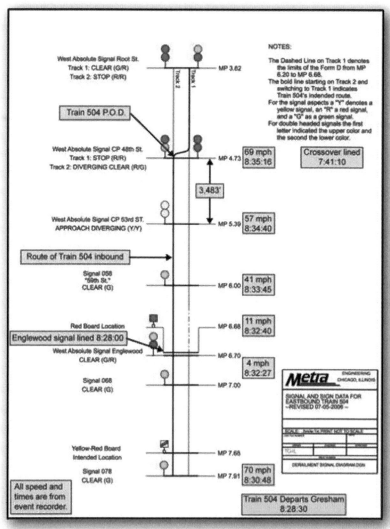

NTSB, DCA-05-MR-013, shows the sequence of signals train 504 should have encountered if in fact train 504 was to cross over from track two to track one.

Point of Derailment (POD). The track warrant showed track work on an upcoming portion of the track, between MP 6.68 and MP 6.2. A Form B, restricting train movements to provide protection for maintenance workers, had been issued for track two, the track that train 504 was on; the restriction was in effect between eight in the morning and five in the evening. Metra procedures required train engineers to contact the employee in charge of the work crew for permission to enter the work limits at the speed specified by the employee in charge.

The train derailed at the milepost 4.7 crossover.

NTSB, DCA-05-MR-013

In testimony to the NTSB, Mr. Smith favorably compared the CSXT practice of assigning both an engineer and a conductor to a train with Metra's lone-engineer system: "Because you are letting the other crew member know what signal indications that you have... And if you, as the engineer, don't act on those indications, then the conductor or other crew member will possibly have an opportunity to take action, you know, maybe even stop, put the train in emergency if you don't act on that indication." he said. "Like, say if it's an approach, you have to reduce speed. Or if it's a stop signal or restricted and you're just continuing on, with that other crew member, he can act." (Board, Railroad Accident Brief DCA-05-MR013, testimony, file documents 2005)

Jeff Thomas of the Federal Railroad Administration was interviewed by the panel established by the NTSB to investigate the September 17, 2005, accident. He worked as a signal and train-control specialist, and had been involved in false proceed investigations in which the train is erroneously signaled to proceed at a higher speed than should be allowed. If the signal aspects were in fact clear at the time of the September 17, 2005, collision, that would have been considered a false proceed. Such incidents may be rare, but they do happen, and the results can be horrific when they do. During the questioning, members of the panel exchanged information about two additional NTSB investigations taking place in the Chicago suburbs, both of which were suspected of being false proceeds, as well as two more collision investigations that featured expert testimony by locomotive engineers and conductors that false proceeds had occurred.

The NTSB's accident report indicated the probable cause and most significant contributing factor was the locomotive engineer's inattentiveness to signal indications and his failure to operate the train in accordance with signal indications and the speed restriction for the crossover at Control Point 48th Street. Contributing to the accident was lack of recognition by Metra of the risk posed by the significant difference between track speed and crossover speed at the accident location and its inaction to reduce that risk through additional operational safety procedures or other means. Also contributing to the accident was the lack of a positive train control system.

Los Angeles, Chatsworth, California

. . .

HEAD-ON COLLISION, SEPTEMBER 12, 2008

AT 4:22 P.M. ON SEPTEMBER 12, 2008, a westbound Metrolink commuter train with a locomotive and three passenger cars traveling at about forty-three mph collided head-on with a Union Pacific eastbound freight train, known as the Leesdale Local, traveling at about forty-one mph. The freight train had two locomotives and was hauling seventeen cars. The Metrolink locomotive was pushed back fifty-two feet into the first passenger car, destroying the car and substantially damaging the two cars behind it. The collision resulted in twenty-five fatalities, with 102 injured passengers taken to local hospitals. Many of those transported to hospitals were in critical condition ("NTSB/RAR-10/01, NTSB PB2010-916301").

Although I had heard media reports of this collision, it was not my intention to either review it in detail or include comments about it in this book. However, at one of our DuPage Railroad Safety Council meetings, I had heard that the Southern California Rail Authority, known as Metrolink, began operating with two engineers instead of the single locomotive engineer it had previously operated with, and that the change was a result of the collision in Chatsworth, CA.

Every locomotive engineer whom I've heard address the subject has voiced the opinion that the commuter rail system would be a much safer system with that important redundancy safety factor.

Freight lines operate with two people in the front end of their trains, a locomotive engineer and a conductor, each alert to dangers, able to stop the train, and required to communicate together about signal aspects as track signals are approached.

The similarities between the Chatsworth collision and the incidents and collisions described in the previous chapters are too great to ignore. Once again, it appeared the NTSB had ignored the lessons learned from history and failed to connect the dots concerning the similarities between the collisions. All had involved track switches, and the NTSB stated that the probable cause in all occurred after the track-signal aspects had been allegedly misread by professional locomotive engineers and conductors sitting in the most dangerous location on their trains. All the incidents had occurred just after the locomotive engineer had increased train speeds as a positive response to the track-signal aspect they thought they had seen.

The collisions resulted in hundreds of injuries, many deaths, millions of dollars in property damage, and the ruin of the professional reputation of many railroad employees. The NTSB ignored eyewitness after eyewitness who stated the signal aspects were read and interpreted correctly.

The Chatsworth collision occurred on a single main track system with a controlled rail siding. The Metrolink commuter train had stopped at the Chatsworth commuter station to service commuters. Slightly less than a mile west of the station, Control Point (CP) Topanga track signals stood about twenty-one feet off the ground with signal lenses of eight and three-eighths inches in diameter. Just west of CP Topanga is a switch to a rail siding for eastbound rail traffic. The siding stretched for 11,300 feet and ran east and parallel to the main track. The track curves dramatically just west of the switch, preventing both westbound and eastbound train engineers from having an unobstructed view of the track beyond the curve. Because of the track curvature, the maximum speed limit in the area of the collision was forty mph.

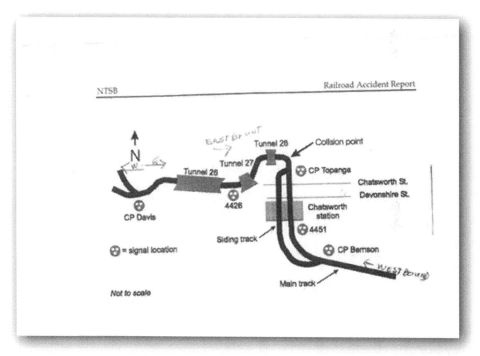

If the signal was operating correctly, Metrolink locomotive engineer Robert Sanchez should have seen a red signal aspect, or stop, given at the CP Topanga track signal from about a mile away, and should have stopped his train east of the CP Topanga track signal. This would have allowed the oncoming freight train to enter the track rail siding at the siding switch.

Based on the Metrolink event recorder's timeline, after leaving the station Mr. Sanchez would have been able to observe the signal aspect for two minutes before having reached the point where he should have stopped his train. Once the UP freight train had completely entered into the siding, and it was safe for the Metrolink to proceed, the train would then have been given a signal to proceed.

The NTSB obtained evidence from Verizon Wireless indicating that Mr. Sanchez had either sent or received many text messages while operating his train in violation of Metrolink policy. One was received about a minute before the collision. Sanchez, forty-seven, was killed in the collision.

The NTSB determined that the *probable cause* of the collision was "the failure of the Metrolink engineer to observe and appropriately respond to the red signal aspect at CP Topanga because he was engaged in the *prohibited* use of a wireless device, specifically text messaging, that distracted him from his duties" (emphasis added).

"Contributing to the accident was the lack of a positive train-control system, which would have stopped the Metrolink train short of the red signal and thus prevented the collision," the NTSB concluded.

On the day of the collision, Mr. Sanchez was working the fifth straight day of his normal split-shift schedule. It called for him to start work at six in the morning, work the morning rush hour until about nine-thirty in the morning, take time off until about two in the afternoon, and conclude his workday at nine o'clock in the evening. He told his conductor he had taken a two-hour nap during his break. Mr. Sanchez was six feet tall and weighed 254 pounds during a company physical exam a month before the collision. He was significantly overweight, had type 2 diabetes, high blood pressure, and was diagnosed HIV-positive two years before the collision. His medications included metformin, glipizide, pioglitazone, benazepril, and antiretroviral medications. All could have negative side effects, and when combined, the results could lead to fatigue, headaches, dizziness, light-headedness, and vision difficulties. Metrolink was aware of many, but not all, of Mr. Sanchez's health issues.

The NTSB determined that Mr. Sanchez's fatigue, medical condition, or medical treatments did not contribute to the collision. The NTSB determined that the signal aspect, which could have been observed for about two minutes by Mr. Sanchez prior to the collision, was missed, that the signal aspect was in fact red, and that Sanchez missed it solely because he was using a wireless device.

Based on their attributing probable cause to locomotive engineer error, the NTSB ruled out operator fatigue, Sanchez's medical condition, and medications as contributing factors. There was frequent use of a wireless device, in violation of company rules, by Mr. Sanchez. He sent his last text message at 4:22:01 p.m.—less than a second before the collision occurred.

According to Metrolink's event recorder, at 4:20:19 p.m., the throttle of the commuter train was increased to its maximum position, the brakes were fully released, and the train was soon traveling at about forty mph. Sanchez was an experienced locomotive engineer, and reacted to a signal aspect he believed to be green by leaving the Chatsworth Station and accelerating his train.

Based only on the very similar fact patterns that existed in this collision and the other accidents, I am inclined to believe the signal aspect was green. The locomotive engineer was killed in the collision. However, four eyewitnesses confirmed that the signal aspect at CP Topanga—the signal governing the movement of the Metrolink train—was green before the train left the Chatsworth Station about two minutes before the collision.

The train's conductor, Robert Heldenbrand, was the only crew member to survive the collision. He had more than ten years of experience as a conductor. Mr. Heldenbrand testified that he stepped off the train from the rear passenger car and onto the Chatsworth platform during the train's fifty-seven second stop in the station. Stepping back into the rear passenger car, he looked down the side of the train, saw the green (clear) signal aspect at the CP Topanga signal, and radioed to the engineer to "highball 111 on a green signal." He was telling Mr. Sanchez to proceed.

A station security guard and two rail fans also saw the CP Topanga signal aspect as the train was leaving the station. All three were standing on the station platform as the train left the station and indicated the signal aspect was green, or clear. "I saw the light was green. Everything seemed all right" said Chris Watson, the security guard at the station. "That light was green" said train buff Bob Atkinson. "He had a full-blown green light when he left," said train buff Chris Cassel. (Hennessy-Fiske, Connell and Lopez 2008)

Connex Railroad, a private contractor that employed and supervised both the engineer and conductor, had suggested that the witness statements cast doubt on the NTSB belief and eventual finding that the signal was red, instead of green, or clear. "They didn't seem to pay much attention to the four eyewitnesses," said Jim Hall, a former NTSB chairman and consultant for Connex. (Lopez and Connell 2010)

The NTSB determined the eyewitnesses were mistaken about the signal aspect.

The article also quoted "William Keppen, a former locomotive engineer and Maryland based railroad consultant, [who] said that false track signals can occur but that they are exceedingly rare. In 13 years as an engineer, he said he encountered false green signals twice, but did not proceed because he knew another train was on the tracks in front of him." (Hennessy-Fiske, Connell and Lopez 2008)

The Chatsworth collision occurred where the track was curved and where the sight line of each engineer would not allow either one to see the other train until just four or five seconds before colliding.

The NTSB collision sign-distance tests found that the first view of the opposing trains by either engineer came when the trains were about 540 feet apart. With both trains traveling at about forty mph, neither train could have stopped in time to avoid the collision.

The CP Topanga signal is high on a post, along straight track, and about a mile from the station. The track began to curve just beyond the signal. During the NTSB's sight-distance testing after the collision, the CP Topanga-signal aspect was seen by an engineer stopped at the Chatsworth Station at about the same place and same time engineer Sanchez had stopped his ill-fated train.

CP Topanga as viewed from the cab of a locomotive positioned at Chatsworth station. Upper arrow indicates approximate location of the CP Topanga signal, which is about 5,288 feet away.

Westbound signal at CP Topanga displaying a red aspect (indicating stop.)

In testimony during the second day of NTSB hearings regarding the Chatsworth collision, William Walpert of the Brotherhood of Locomotive Engineers and Trainmen addressed the safety impact of assigning two people to a train's locomotive or control cab car. "There are occasions where something's going to happen. A second set of eyes, in our opinion, would go a long way in preventing accidents," (Union Recommends 2 Workers in All Train Cabs 2009)

The article continues: "Kitty Higgins, an NTSB board member, expressed doubts about the union's recommendation, pointing out that a accident involving another Metrolink train occurred weeks after the deadly September crash and the implementation of the new policy of having a second worker in the control cab car.

"I can understand from the unions' standpoint why they would like more employees driving these trains, but from a safety standpoint, I think the jury's still out as to whether that's the formula for solving the problem," Higgins said. (Union Recommends 2 Workers in All Train Cabs 2009)

Prior to the Chatsworth collision, the NTSB had faulted rail service locomotive engineers for missing signal aspects in four similar incidents that I reviewed. In three of the incidents, as in the Chatsworth collision, there was only one person in the control cab car of the train. Over the years, engineer after engineer has testified that commuter rail safety might be improved with another person in the front end of the train who can help to operate it. Two people in the front end of the train would not eliminate all train collisions, but would reduce the probability of one occurring and better manage risk. With more than thirty years of high-level government service at the time of the Chatsworth collision, Board Member Higgins should have realized that the jury had been in for many years.

In each of the five commuter rail incidents investigated by the NTSB—the Placentia head-on, the Aurora head-on, the derailment at milepost 4.7 on the Rock Island, the second derailment on the same line at the same milepost, and the Chatsworth collision—the NTSB indicated that the most significant contributing factor was loss of situational awareness leading to missed or misinterpreted signal aspects by the locomotive engineers and conductors.

Elmwood Park Collision

. . .

November 23, 2005

Elmwood Park, Illinois, is a suburb just west of Chicago. Through it runs a busy Metra three-track system. Most of the way through town, the tracks run parallel with Grand Avenue, a busy four-lane street that averages 20,900 vehicles every weekday. At one point, the train tracks curve and cross Grand Avenue (DOT/AAR 372131E) on a diagonal, making this one of the widest crossings in Illinois at 366 feet. (Board, Highway Accident Report HWY-06-MH-007 2005)

On Thanksgiving eve (one of the busiest travel days of the year), November 23, 2005, at the Grand Avenue crossing, a Metra/NIRC commuter train struck six vehicles, which in turn struck other vehicles that were backed up on the tracks.

At the time, the Grand Avenue crossing was one of the most accident-prone crossings in Illinois, and still, commuter trains were allowed to travel over the crossing at seventy mph, while freight trains could only travel through the crossing at thirty mph. Between 1956 and November 2005, there had been forty-five collisions at the crossing, resulting in seven fatalities and twenty-seven injuries. The previous train-versus-vehicle collision had been on another Thanksgiving eve, November 24, 2004, the year before, and had caused two injuries. Westbound commuter trains' locomotive engineers traveling from Chicago normally have a very short line of sight, about 450 feet, to the approaching Grand Avenue crossing.

When Metra locomotive engineer Wayne Lumpkins approached the crossing at the height of evening rush hour at just before 4:43 p.m., his westbound train was traveling at seventy mph, or just over one hundred feet per second. His line of sight to the crossing was about 450 feet. When he saw vehicles on the tracks, he attempted to stop his train, but his train was still traveling at sixty-five mph when it collided with six vehicles stopped on the tracks. These vehicles were pushed into other vehicles. A total of eighteen vehicles were either destroyed or sustained damages and fifteen people were injured, but fortunately there were no deaths.

In a newspaper article after the 2005 collision, locomotive engineer Lumpkins indicated that this was not the first time he had seen cars on the tracks as his train approached the Elmwood Park crossing. "This happens all the time." (Groark 2005)

After the accident, Metra reduced the maximum speed of the commuter trains at the crossing to thirty mph. When I walked the collision site in July 2012, I saw a Metra employee and asked him if the crossing was safer at the lower speed. He indicated it was much safer, and that now, vehicles have time to move off the tracks.

When I met Dennis Mogan in 2012, who was Metra's director of safety and rules at the time of the 2005 Elmwood Park incident, we talked about Elmwood Park, where the train speed limit had been reduced to thirty mph following the 2005 Thanksgiving eve collision. (Mogan 2012)

The NTSB, in its final report on this collision, did not mention the train's high speed at this curved and short line-of-sight crossing as contributing factors.

The Elmwood Park incident is a tragic example of a commuter train traveling too fast at a dangerous crossing in an urban area. In a crowded urban setting like Chicago and its suburbs, streets and traffic signals are often located within feet of busy rail grade crossings. Some crossings are far more dangerous than others.

When comparing the stopping distance of a train at different speeds, the equation used is not linear, but exponential. For example, if it would take a train traveling at seventy mph about twenty-four hundred feet to stop by using emergency braking, then at fifty mph, the same train's stopping distance using the same braking process would be reduced to about twelve hundred feet, and it would take more time to reach the crossing if braking at the lower speed than it would take at the same distance from the crossing at the higher speed.

After the Fox River Grove, October 25, 1995, collision that involved a Metra/UP commuter train and a school bus, local residents protested the seventy mph speeds. Metra—after first arguing that the speed didn't affect safety—decided to permanently reduce the maximum speed at that crossing to fifty mph.

The *Chicago Tribune*, in an editorial, felt that lowering the train speeds was not a solution and wrote, "Slowing the trains may bring satisfaction to the good people of Fox River Grove, but it won't solve the problem." (Editorial, Slower trains aren't the answer 1997)

My response was published in the *Tribune's* August 15, 1997, edition as a letter to the editor, "Gov. Jim Edgar recently signed a bill that reduces Metra commuter train speeds from 70 mph to 50 mph in Fox River Grove for a three-year test period…Lowering Metra train speeds at highly congested grade crossings to 50 mph will save lives. To confine this test to Fox River Grove defies logic and common sense. The test should be system-wide." (Swimmer, Lower Train Speeds Can Save Lives 1997)

The NTSB accident report stated the following as to probable cause:

> The National Transportation Safety Board determines that the probable cause of the Elmwood Park accident was a combination of factors that led to the development of a traffic queue on the West Grand Avenue highway-rail grade crossing and prevented queued vehicles from exiting the crossing prior to the arrival of a Northeast Illinois Regional Commuter Railroad (METRA) train: the factors were the acute angle of intersection between West Grand Avenue and the railroad tracks, which resulted in an exceptionally wide grade crossing; the unusually heavy vehicle traffic that preceded the Thanksgiving holiday; and the complex street and rail pattern and related signal interactions between Harlem Avenue and the West Grand Avenue grade crossing, which frequently desynchronized the traffic signals along West Grand Avenue during peak travel times.

The NTSB accident report did not indicate that a contributing factor was that the train was traveling too fast for conditions.

Lunch with Dennis Mogan

. . .

When we met for lunch in 2012 at Portillo's Hot Dogs in Streamwood, Illinois, it had been some years since Dennis Mogan and I had last talked. Dennis and I were two of the DuPage Railroad Safety Council's founding members. Dennis was an experienced locomotive engineer with many years of railroading experience. When we first met, he was Metra's director of safety and rules. At lunch, Dennis said he had left Metra some years earlier, worked with the NTSB for a while and was now a railroad inspector for the Illinois Commerce Commission.

As a volunteer member of the DRSC, Dennis was elected vice-chairman of our group, attended monthly Saturday meetings, and was involved in other DRSC activities. As Metra's director of safety and rules, he was involved in the investigation of all Metra incidents, including train derailments and highway rail crossing collisions. In the major Metra collisions investigated by the NTSB, Mr. Mogan worked side by side with NTSB investigators and was part of their investigative team. He participated as a panel member at NTSB hearings, interviewing those directly involved in the collision as well as other witnesses.

Before meeting with Mr. Mogan, I e-mailed Lanny Wilson, DRSC chairman, to tell him I thought the NTSB may have erred in finding that operator error was the most significant contributing factor in three major Chicago-area Metra incidents. Lanny suggested I contact Dennis Mogan. I had thought of contacting Dennis, but felt he would not want to talk with me about a book I was writing that would be critical of Metra, the NTSB, the FRA, and others. When I contacted Dennis, he seemed curious, so we met for lunch and had an open and candid hour and a half discussion of various issues I wanted to address in this book. He responded to each one of my questions, comments, or conclusions. His comments were candid and on point.

Dennis believed the June 12, 2002, Aurora head-on collision was caused by missed signals. As part of the investigation, he had sat in a train stopped in the exact spot as the train that had been involved in the collision. He sat in the coach seats where the locomotive engineer and the off-duty conductor deadheading into Chicago would have sat. Dennis said the track signal was not visible from either seat.

The on-duty conductor, who was not in the control cab car, had indicated the track signal aspect was green and that the train could leave the station with two buzzes to the locomotive engineer. Dennis said the conductor's buzzes were more of an automatic reaction to the expected signal aspect, adding that he believed the actual signal aspect was red, not green, meaning the train should not have left the station.

I asked Dennis if there was a track signal at the nearby crossover that the engineer could have seen and relied on. He said there was no track signal, but the engineer should have seen that the crossover wasn't aligned, and the train should not have proceeded past it. When I suggested the engineer had been doing safety tests when the train was leaving the station, and that this may have distracted him from looking at the tracks, he agreed.

At about this point, I stated my belief that there should be two people in the locomotive or control cab car operating the train. **Dennis told me he had asked Metra fifteen years earlier to bring the conductor into the locomotive or control cab car and add another ticket-taker to the train crew. Metra wouldn't do it, he said, and still has not done so.** Without exception, everyone I know with experience as a Metra locomotive engineer believes such a change would dramatically improve Metra's safety record. Redundancy and an extra set of eyes are key concepts in transportation safety. Where they exist, safer operations also exist.

However, it was a different story as we talked about the derailments of October 12, 2003, and September 17, 2005, at milepost 4.7 on the Metra Rock Island Line that stretches from Chicago's LaSalle Street Station to Joliet, IL. As we talked through the details and similarities of the two collisions, Dennis began to agree that there may have been anomalies with the signal system—that the track signals may have shown green/clear signal aspects just as the locomotive engineers had stated. Dennis indicated that the signals at the crossover for milepost 4.7 were comprised of both hard-wire leads and wireless microprocessors, and a power surge could have created a clear signal that could not be duplicated in subsequent tests.

In August 2013, the FRA came out with an unusual press release that was widely noticed by the Chicago media. It started out with "The Federal Railroad Administration (FRA) has the authority and the responsibility to provide safety oversight on the Northeast Illinois Regional Commuter Railroad (Metra)." The release followed with seven elements in the FRA's Oversight Plan.

Five dealt with increased meetings and more communication between the FRA, Metra employees, and labor representatives. One dealt with FRA inspectors increasing the number of inspections on Metra trains, including FRA inspectors riding in the locomotive cab with the Metra engineer and "observing his operation of the train, his overall knowledge of operating rules, and his awareness of the operating environment." One included, "FRA inspectors will increase oversight of Metra's operational test and inspection program."

The press release states that the reason for the oversight plan is because Metra has experienced some changes in leadership; however, "FRA inspection results show that Metra continues to be a safe and efficient operation." (Administration, FRA Oversight Plan for Northeast Illinois Regional Commuter Railroad 2013)

In a letter to US senator Dick Durbin from Illinois, FRA administrator Joseph Szabo stated the agency intends to conduct "regular inspections of Metra tracks, signals, and operations to establish compliance with federal regulations of railroads." (Wronski, Federal Agency Bolsters It Oversight of Metra 2003)

FRA collision statistics raise concerns about Metra. In my opinion, Metra is involved in far too many collisions. They have a history of ignoring signal inspection requirements, they overwork their employees, and they punish employees who speak out about safety concerns.

Mr. Mogan went on to tell of a false proceed signal-aspect malfunction that appeared when a train in which a supervisor from the Metra's signal unit was riding along with the train's operating engineer in the locomotive. The train was following another train through a crossover. The lead train also had a signal person riding along with that train's locomotive engineer. If the following train had proceeded as the signal aspects indicated, it would have collided with the back of the lead train as it went through the crossover.

I told Dennis that up until the October 12, 2003, derailment at Forty-Seventh Street, according to testimony given on December 17, 2003 when a panel established on behalf of NTSB interviewed David Rodriquez, senior manager of train operations for Metra, Metra had not compiled statistical information about signal malfunctions and repairs. The NTSB started the questioning of David Rodriquez by indicating the NTSB had requested signal trouble reports from Metra and hadn't received these records. There had been testimony that the information had been contained on daily train sheets, but that it hadn't been compiled into a database and hadn't been used as a statistical tool to help determine the various types of signal problems, and where these problems had been occurring. "NTSB investigative report, October 12, 2003," incident testimony received through Freedom of Information Act. (Board, NTSB/RAR-05-03, PB2005-916303, Notation 7615A 2005)

I indicated that the NTSB should have gone back at least five years to compile this information for meaningful statistical analysis. Dennis said that would probably have been next to impossible because notations about signal malfunctions were scribbled almost anywhere, including the back of a daily train sheet. Even so, I thought it may have shed some light on the frequency, the location, and the type of malfunctions reported.

I also told Dennis the NTSB should have talked with other active locomotive engineers and conductors to see if they had experienced signal malfunctions. The NTSB had not done this. Dennis seemed to agree.

He said that running relatively inexperienced locomotive engineers on different Metra routes, which Metra frequently does, was unsafe. He referred me to the Amtrak and Norfolk Southern collision of November 30, 2007. The NTSB findings determined that a significant contributing factor was the Amtrak locomotive engineer's confusion about the meanings of the signal aspects because his route covered four different rail lines, and the same signal aspect meant something different on each. The same problem also exists when Metra locomotive engineers move from one commuter line to another within Metra's rail system. The danger is compounded when inexperienced engineers are moved from district to district.

We talked about the Fox River Grove collision in which a Metra/ UP train collided with a school bus on October 25, 1995. I told Dennis that I had disagreed with the NTSB's final accident report, which should have included the engineer's operator fatigue as a contributing factor.

Metra locomotive engineer Ford Dotson Jr. testified that he had seen the bus moving across the grade crossing at about twenty-two seconds from the crossing and thought he had started to stop the train at that point. However, the train's event recorder and a subsequent NTSB controlled reenactment after the collision showed the train's stopping process began much later than twenty-two seconds from the crossing. These delayed reactions, and thinking you are doing something faster than you actually are, are classic symptoms of fatigue. I now believe he reacted when he first saw the train moving across the tracks. However, he hadn't realized he was as close to the crossing as he was. The lack of situational awareness is also a sign of fatigue.

Dennis and I went over Dotson's lengthy commute to work, when he woke up, and when he arrived home after a long split-shift day.

When I mentioned that Dotson had testified that he regularly slept four hours at Metra's layover facility between his morning and afternoon runs, Dennis shook his head and indicated that the facilities aren't really conducive for sleeping, let alone sleeping soundly, for four-hour stretches. Like me, Dennis doubted that Dotson had slept continuously and soundly between his morning and afternoon runs.

Even if Dotson had slept as he'd indicated he had, fatigue was inevitable, I contended. The NTSB seemed to take Dotson at his word without talking with others familiar with the layover sleep facilities provided by Metra. These layover sleep facilities are a problem. From what I had heard from other locomotive engineers, it is a fairly common practice for engineers not to sleep during their layover periods.

If the NTSB had indicated fatigue as a contributing factor to the collision, a solid argument could have been made for more continuous off hours, a reduction in total hours worked, better resting and sleeping conditions between the split shifts, shorter driving times to and from work, and for two people to be assigned to the cab end of the train.

The Fox River Grove incident had occurred more than fifteen years earlier. I believe Metra locomotive engineers still work far too many split-shift hours and then remain alone in the locomotive compartment operating their trains. According to FRA data, nationally, train collisions had decreased over the last fifteen years by 34 percent, from 2,771 in 1999 to 1,813 in 2013, while Metra's accident record has not followed that pattern and had in fact increased.

Dennis and I talked also about ten-year-old Michael DeLarco's death at River Grove on February 23, 2004. After the collision, at Mr. Mogan's recommendation, Metra fired several engineers involved in the collision for not following Metra's rules relating to how commuter trains can approach a commuter station when there is another train either in that station or in the process of exiting that station, and when a train can exit a commuter station and leave it unprotected when another train is approaching. Sometime after their firing, a federal arbitrator ruled against Metra, saying it didn't follow *due process* in firing the engineers, and they were allowed to return to work with back pay.

Some form of the hold out special instructions to train engineers exists on all Metra routes except one. The lone exception is the BNSF line. Dennis and I agreed that the BNSF line should have some way of better protecting commuters and others from second-train accidents at or near a station. I believe far too many such collisions have occurred along the BNSF commuter line. Dennis said there is an Illinois regulation that requires trains to sound their horns when they are approaching one another at a station, even in a quiet zone. This regulation too often is not followed, he said.

We also talked about the Elmwood Park Thanksgiving eve collision, where the train speed limit had been reduced to thirty mph following the collision. Dennis said the speed of trains at the crossing had been reduced at his direction.

In one Metra derailment (see "Derailment at Milepost 4.7 #2,") investigated by the NTSB, a locomotive engineer's employment record at another railroad, which contained notations of several rule infractions, was not included in his work record that was reviewed by Metra when the engineer was hired by Metra. Only some portions of the locomotive engineer's work history currently follow the engineer from railroad to railroad as he or she changes employment. Dennis felt strongly that the complete work history from all railroads should follow a locomotive engineer from one railroad to another, much as a commercial airline pilot's complete work record follows the pilot from one airline to another.

When I asked about Metra railroad officials and union officials being made part of the NTSB investigative teams and potentially influencing an investigation that is being represented as independent, Dennis said the end result is not influenced by this close relationship.

We also talked about Metra's former chief executive officer, Phil Pagano, who committed suicide in 2010 by stepping in front of a Metra train. At the time of his death, Pagano was being investigated for financial improprieties. On the day of his death, he was to attend a Metra board meeting where he was expected to be fired. He had been Metra's CEO for some twenty years.

When I told Dennis I thought the Metra board had placed way too much confidence in Pagano and essentially allowed him to run Metra as he saw fit, Dennis agreed. He pointed out that the board members were political appointees and, as a group, had little railroading background. (Mogan 2012)

Lunch with Lanny Wilson

· · ·

MARCH 20, 2013 WAS CERTAINLY too cold for golf, and on this day the Hinsdale Golf Club was almost empty. Lanny Wilson had invited me to lunch at the club several weeks earlier. I had asked Lanny if I could interview him for my book. The Hinsdale Golf club is a beautiful, mature, older course with a stately clubhouse.

Lanny, who like me, enjoys writing, had written an article that he had e-mailed to me several days earlier about how important heartfelt emotions are. That was how I wanted to close this book, with heartfelt emotions.

As the luncheon started, I mentioned how friendly the staff at the club was and asked how long he had been a member. Lanny had joined the club when his daughter Lauren was eleven. When he joined, he had thought that it would be a beautiful place to someday hold her wedding. Lauren was killed several years later at the Monroe Street crossing in Hinsdale, when she was fourteen.

Lanny went on to tell me what has directed him toward improving rail safety. His son was the driver of the car and was seriously injured in the 1994 collision that resulted in Lauren's death. As he was visiting his son at the hospital, his friend and fellow member of his church, Ellie Goers was also in the room visiting. Ellic's son Jonathan had been injured at the same Monroe Street crossing about four years earlier. Ellie commented that if she had done something to improve rail safety after Jonathan's collision, then maybe Lauren's collision would not have occurred. Upon hearing those comments, Lanny knew that he would actively work to improve rail safety.

When I last saw Ellie Goers at a railroad safety event in late 2012, she was telling me of her daughter's recent wedding and how Jonathan was brought from his permanent care facility to attend the wedding. I could tell that the wedding and the fact that Jonathan attended was a very special and wonderful event for the Goers.

At the luncheon, Lanny and I talked about the collision in which Lauren was killed. Her seventeen-year-old brother was driving west on a street south of and parallel to the railroad tracks. He saw the westbound Metra commuter train and raced the train for several blocks as he tried to beat it to the crossing. He went around the activated downed gates at Monroe Street and his car was struck by the train.

Lanny went on to say that, just several days before the collision, his son was taken off a medication that had been prescribed for attention deficit disorder. When I asked if his son had been on Ritalin, he said no, but that it was similar. His son was seriously injured in the collision, both physically and emotionally. Although Lanny's son married several years ago, he lacks confidence and has trouble meeting and interacting with people. His son does not talk about the collision.

Linnea Wilson, Lanny's wife and the mother of Lauren and her brother, entered the seminary after the collision and is now a practicing minister. She does not talk about the collision.

Lanny Wilson is not only chairman of the DuPage Railroad Safety Council but is also vice-president of the DuPage County Medical Board. I remember at a DRSC meeting years ago when he mentioned that he had recently delivered his five thousandth baby.

He writes articles for his church paper and hopes to write a book. In one of his writings titled "I Sent You" he writes of watching the weekly TV show *Face the Nation* hosted by Bob Schieffer. Schieffer was interviewing Rabbi David Wolf, who shared the following insight: "When I teach the kids in my school, I always tell them this story about a kid who looks up at the heavens, and says, 'Dear God, there's so much suffering and pain and anguish in the world. Why don't you send help?' and God says, 'I did send help. I sent you.'" (Wilson 2013)

When I asked how Linnea and Lanny were able to stay together after Lauren's death and their son's injuries, Lanny said that, in their sorrow, they each needed someone to hold on to.

In a newspaper article that appeared shortly after the collision, the following quote appeared: "I saw Lauren as somebody who really wanted to give of herself," said Hinsdale Central counselor Richard Quaintance. "She got things done. She had a charisma that comes from a natural blend of intelligence, leadership and genuine concern for the rights and feelings of others." (Gottesmann 1994)

After the luncheon with Lanny, I traveled the route his son would have traveled down Hinsdale Avenue when he was racing the train. The locomotive engineer, from where he operated the Metra train, would have neither seen the car nor sensed the danger until it was too late to react to avoid the collision. Would an additional person helping to operate the train, sitting in a position with a clear view of the parallel street running just feet south of the tracks, have seen the racing car, sensed danger at the approaching crossing, and reacted in a timely manner? No one can answer that, although one locomotive engineer told me it is fairly common for cars to race trains when driving on a parallel road.

Trespassing

. . .

When the DRSC was formed, it took the position that in order to improve rail safety, whether at crossings or at other places along the tracks, it is essential that people be deterred from doing thoughtless, foolish, and dangerous activities, and in doing so, we in turn are managing risk better.

We also learned early on from one of the railroad people in our group that it is important to focus on the three E's: enforcement, engineering, and education.

In the early days of the DRSC, the mid-1990s, I was essentially a one-person subcommittee investigating Chicago-area railroad accidents at grade crossings and those that involved trespassers who were not at grade crossings. There was one common thread in the pattern of the trespassing incidents that I investigated. There was always easy access to railroad tracks. In all cases I investigated, there was either no fencing, or when fencing existed, which was seldom, it was on private property and in disrepair, with gaping holes making it both easy and inviting for a person to walk through. Most often, by its appearance, the fencing had been in disrepair for years.

In the period from 1975 through 1994, there were over 9,000 trespassing fatalities in the United States. Trespassing incidents were occurring frequently in Chicago and its suburban areas.

Often, these train-versus-trespasser accidents were near schools, parks, or well-worn shortcut paths over the tracks. Far too often they involved young people. At one of our early DRSC meetings, Debbie Hare, who at the time worked in management at Amtrak, said that whenever she heard that Amtrak was involved in a trespassing incident, she was almost certain that a young person would be the person killed or injured.

Soon I learned the term "hot spots" that was used by railroad locomotive engineers and other railroad people to refer to illegal crossings most often used by trespassers. These "hot spots" were well-known by the train crews that operated on those tracks.

One such "hot spot" was in Naperville. There are two parks, Burlington Park and Heritage Woods, and the only separation between these two parks is a very busy three track BNSF rail system. There was no fencing, and to add further risk to an already dangerous environment, there was a train trestle going over a nearby river. On the shore underneath the tracks were scattered many beer cans. Surely, it was a hangout for young people.

Another "hot spot" I went to was a busy set of tracks running next to Fenton High School in Bensenville. The high school sits on the south side of the tracks. I first visited the area almost twenty years ago and returned to visit recently. Not much if anything had changed. There is a fence next to the high school's various athletic fields, but the fence does not encircle the fields, and it is easy for students crossing the tracks to enter the school grounds. On the private property north of the tracks, there is either no fencing, or whatever few fences existed seemed to be in disrepair. The railroad had not put up fencing on their property.

In a well-written and lengthy article called "When death rides the rails" by *Chicago Tribune's* Jon Hilkevitch, dated July 4, 2004, the author interviews Chicago-area train crews about fatal collisions that their trains had been involved in. The article dealt with the emotional upheaval these railroad train crews feel when a fatal collision occurs. In the article, he writes of a train crew member who had to detrain and walk to the body of a person whose death had been ruled a suicide. Hilkevitch writes,

> Metra assistant conductor Rick Hodges, the first to reach Wojcicki's body, remains haunted as well. Revisiting the death scene some weeks later with a Tribune reporter, he eyed the hulking outlines of Fenton High School just across the athletic field from the tracks. Painted on the Route 83 overpass where Wojcicki awaited the train is the Fenton mascot and greeting, Welcome to Bison Country.
>
> Hodges was thinking about the students he sees each day putting themselves at risk by short-cutting across the tracks and smoking cigarettes underneath the bridge. A well-worn path leads from the school's sports field, up the embankment to the tracks and down the other side. At least four fatalities have occurred at the location in recent years, authorities say.

At DRSC meetings, we talked about the many trespassing incidents not only in the Chicago area but throughout the country. We all seemed to agree that railroads' justification for not installing fencing at known "hot spots" was inadequate. Even when the railroads posted No Trespassing signs on to their private property, far too many trespassing incidents were taking place. The signs were often simply ignored by trespassers, many of whom were young people, as they often crossed the tracks at well-worn and well-known "hot spot" footpaths. Private property owners, for whatever reason, either did not put up fencing since they were not legally obligated to install it, or, when they did, often left it in disrepair.

Some of the comments heard at the DRSC meetings in the mid-1990s were: if the railroads put up fencing, and it is cut and not repaired on a timely basis, their exposure increases if a lawsuit occurs; there are thorny bushes that can be grown along the tracks that can work as good if not better than fencing.

In 1996 I wrote a letter to the editor that was published by many Chicago and suburban papers, including the *Chicago Tribune*, the *Daily Herald*, and the *Chicago Sun-Times*. The letter is as meaningful now in 2015 as it was nineteen years ago.

In Illinois, a concerted effort is underway to reduce one classification of railroad accidents: those at grade crossings.

New laws, more enforcement, improved engineering and more education seem to be helping. Recent Illinois statistics indicate [that] the number of fatal railroad crossing accidents [is] starting to go down. Community leaders, police officers, railroad personnel, educators and concerned citizens deserve a pat on the back for their efforts.

There is, however, another classification of railroad accidents that also deserves immediate attention. These are accidents that take place on railroad property between trains and trespassers. In this country during the last 20 years, more than 9,000 people have been killed by trains in trespass accidents. Many killed were children, teenagers, or young adults who attempted to take a shortcut. In suburban areas, many schools, parks, pools and other attractive nuisances are located within feet of very busy railroad tracks. In many cases, there are no safety fences or other barriers along these very dangerous tracks.

Children, teenagers, and others frequently trespass onto railroad property. Often, they cross the tracks without incident. Many times, however, their luck runs out. Just a few of these many Chicagoland locations are Bensenville's Fenton High School, Downers Grove's Gilbert Park, Hinsdale's community pool and Naperville's Burlington Park. A complete list of Chicagoland's attractive nuisance locations would probably cover several pages.

Illinois does not have a law requiring railroads to install and maintain safety fencing, and railroads are in effect punished for doing so. It cost railroads substantial sums to install and maintain this fencing. If cut, and it often is, there may be increased exposure in a lawsuit. It is easier and less costly for railroads to put up "no trespassing" signs. Safety experts know signs by themselves do little to stop trespassers and are merely ways of reducing the railroads' legal exposure.

Railroads, by law, should be required to install and maintain safety fencing at attractive nuisance locations, and they should be rewarded for doing so, either through tax credits, direct grants or by other means. In Illinois, farmers are required to have fencing up so animals don't stray onto railroad tracks.

It is our moral responsibility to protect our children and young people from known and obvious dangers. It should be the railroads' legal responsibility to do the same.

(Swimmer, Safety fences needed near railroads 1996)

Prior to July 1996, I had sent letters to the then FRA administrator Jolene Molitoris about railroad safety concerns other than trespassing. As administrator she was the chief executive officer of the Federal Railroad Administration.

Her responses had been friendly, timely, and informative. On July 10, 1996, I wrote the following letter to her that in part expressed my concerns about the dangers of trespassing, and enclosed a copy of my letter to the editor: "As you indicated at your nomination hearing, if we are to reduce trespass accidents, we have to come up with new strategies. Hopefully, the enclosed "letter to the editor" will be of interest."

On February 25, 1998, FRA administrator Jolene M. Molitoris, in testimony before a US Senate Subcommittee on Surface Transportation and Merchant Marines stated, "In 1997, trespasser fatalities for the first time clearly eclipsed highway rail crossing fatalities as the largest single component of fatalities in railroad operations. We currently project that trespasser fatalities will rise 13% from 471 reported in 1996 to 530 in 1997."

With that said, FRA Administrator Molitoris went on: "In 1998, FRA will put renewed emphasis on finding solutions that will fit [the] many forms in which [they appear]. Unlike many other railroad safety problems, trespassing is very much a local and regional issue that requires targeted solutions. This is a problem that in various parts of our nation involves [the] homeless, immigrants, children and other dimensions. It is also a problem made worse when media make it appear that the tracks are a place for recreation. We are seeking to address each of these elements of the problem."

In the mid-1990s, those of us involved in railroad safety issues knew of the dangers of trespassing. The railroads certainly knew of these dangers. High-level federal government and elected officials knew of the dangers. I would think that many in the general public were also aware of the dangers. That was almost twenty years ago, and I am saddened to report that very little has been done to reduce trespass incidents on railroad tracks. The number of fatalities and injuries that resulted from railroad collisions at grade crossings has dramatically decreased in the twenty-year period ending in 2013.

An excellent article, "Report: Pedestrian Rail Deaths Get Little Notice," one in a series of articles relating to railroad safety issues written by Todd C. Frankel, *St. Louis Post-Dispatch*, December 23, 2012, follows:

ST. LOUIS (AP)—Around midnight on May 30, Mary Gaffney, 17, was struck and killed by a freight train in Riverdale Park, Md. She was taking a shortcut through a residential area and may have been wearing earphones when a CSX freight train approached rapidly from behind.

She was the fourth person killed walking on the nation's railroad tracks that day. The others were killed in San Mateo, Calif., and the suburbs of Chicago and St. Louis.

What even federal regulators could not see because of how these accidents were reported was that Mary was the fourth pedestrian in less than three years to die on the same stretch of tracks.

Pedestrian railroad accidents typically receive little attention, despite being the leading cause of death on the rails. Since 1997 more than 7,200 pedestrians have been fatally struck and 6,400 have been injured by trains in the United States.

Despite about 500 deaths each year, railroad companies across the country often refuse to take even small steps to deal with the problem, a *St. Louis Post-Dispatch* investigation found.

"Railroads don't want any legal exposure, so they don't accept any responsibility," said Harvey Levine, a former vice president of the Association of American Railroads, who toward the end of his career with the trade group became alarmed by the industry's safety record.

To the railroads, the solution is simple: "The incidents would have been avoided if the persons were not trespassing on railroad property," Union Pacific spokesman Mark Davis said.

It took years of effort to tackle what was once the leading killer on the railroad: highway grade crossings. Following a public outcry in the early 1970s, hundreds of millions of taxpayer dollars were spent to fortify crossings with flashing lights and automatic gates. The result: Crossing accidents have plummeted 80 percent.

But state and federal officials mostly lack powers to require safety improvements to stop people from walking on the tracks. In fact, many states have stricter rules on keeping livestock off the rails than people, leading to the odd scenario where a railroad could be liable for a fatality if it's a calf, but not a child.

A few years ago, the Federal Railroad Administration asked the railroads for internal trespassing reports to get a better sense of who was walking on the tracks. The railroads refused, and the agency recently conceded defeat.

For years, the agency required railroads to report only the county of a death or injury, making it hard to identify hot spots for trespassing, said Ron Ries, director of the agency's Highway-Rail Grade Crossing Safety and Trespass Prevention Division.

In 2008, the agency pushed to require GPS coordinates. The industry objected. But five unions representing railroad workers and state railroad regulators supported the move. And in June 2011, the new federal rule on GPS coordinates took effect. But at least four more years of the data are needed before researchers can even begin to identify trespassing hot spots, says the FRA.

In the meantime, even travel through places with known trespassing risks does not affect track speed limits, which are set by the FRA. Sometimes, even what is happening directly on the tracks doesn't seem to matter.

After two girls were killed on a trestle in Kent, Wash., an Amtrak supervisor testified in 2003 that trains operate with an "inherent right" to go the posted track speed. In that case, the Amtrak engineer had been warned five minutes before the crash by a passing freight train that two girls were playing up ahead.

As the train bore down, the girls, one of whom had cerebral palsy, were running to get off the trestle. With a track limit of 80 mph, the train slowed from 79 to 65 mph, according to court records. The emergency brakes were never applied. Rachel Marturello, 11, and Zandra Lafley, 13, died a few feet from safety.

Asked recently about the Kent case, a spokesman said all Amtrak engineers operate in compliance with federal regulations.

Education is one way to address the trespassing problem, say railroads and regulators. That happens mostly through Operation Lifesaver, a national nonprofit that spreads the message about rail safety. But, the railroad industry is giving less money to state groups and providing fewer employees to help, documents show.

Illinois and Kansas have increased the number of presentations in recent years. But dramatic declines were reported in Missouri, Ohio, New Jersey, Florida, California and

Maryland, according to 2002–2010 data submitted to the national office of Operation Lifesaver.

Joyce Rose, national president, acknowledged the loss of railroad workers, but said the organization remains active "even with all the funding challenges," reaching an average of 1 million people each year since 2005.

Another tool is trespassing arrests. But the railroads employ relatively few police officers and many local police agencies are already spread thin.

The third tool is engineering—restricting access to the tracks using things like fences or overpasses.

Railroads dismiss fencing because, they say, people determined to cross will do it, such as in cases of suicide. They also respond that they can't fence the entire system. "It's impractical to do that," said Robin Chapman, a spokesman for Norfolk Southern.

This is a popular sentiment echoed across the industry. But the call for fencing is a long known problem area. "That is not the same as fencing in 10,000 miles of track," said David Clarke, director at the University of Tennessee's Transportation Research Center.

In Villa Park, Ill., it took a young teen to get a fence built. By age 15, Tiffany Davis had lost two friends in two years to the tracks in this small Chicago suburb.

Trackside memorials dot the rails, including a wood cross marking the spot where a middle school student was killed and two others injured as they walked home from school years ago.

Today, a black, metal rail fence runs along stretches of the tracks, paid for with railroad and public funds. And it seems to be doing its job, local officials say.

Villa Park police officer William Lyons, who investigates train accidents, boasted this fall that it had been 18 months since someone died on the tracks in his town.

It was the longest such streak in years. (Frankel 2012)

For twenty some years, I have heard the railroads say that it is their property and that No Trespassing signs are adequate risk management. I have seen a glorification of trespassing on rail tracks in movies, TV shows, and advertising. There is little proactive enforcement of trespassing violations by policing powers, including railroad police.

If we keep doing the same thing over and over again, which is essentially ignoring such a clear and present danger, it would be foolish not to expect the same results. In the next twenty years, thousands more will be killed and injured. How upsetting, frustrating, and disheartening.

In 2013 the top four US Class 1 railroad freight lines of Union Pacific, BNSF, CSX, and Norfolk Southern, had a combined net income of almost twelve billion dollars. Hopefully, in future years, more monies can be budgeted to restricting trespassers from entering onto railroad tracks, particularly at hot spots.

Kristine Topel

. . .

KRISTIE TOPEL, TWENTY, WAS STRUCK and fatally injured by a Metra commuter train on June 14, 2011, at 12:55 a.m. Published reports of this accident didn't say much, and that would be expected. Train accidents, especially those involving trespassers, are somewhat of a nonmedia event in Illinois, because they occur frequently.

On August, 14, 2014, I met with her parents, Kurt and Laura Topel, in their home. Both are fairly new members of the DRSC group. Their prime focus is the reduction of trespassing fatalities and injuries that occur on railroad tracks. I had gone back and forth on whether to include a chapter or so on trespassing. Trespassing incidents is one area of railroad safety that has frustrated safety advocates for years. After listening to the Topels speak at our meetings, I knew the book would be seriously lacking if the trespassing issue were not addressed.

When we met, Kurt and Laura spoke of their daughter, the accident, rail safety, and trespassing issues. Within minutes after leaving their home, I pulled my car over and sent them an e-mail. In it, I expressed the hope that my words would be able to express how I felt about Kristie. "What a charming young lady," I wrote. What I did not say, but had also learned, was that not only was Kristie charming but she also was strong willed; she was both athletic and adventurous, she was not afraid to step out of her comfort zone, and she was a generous giver of her time to help others.

Many of the specific circumstances leading to Kristie's being fatally injured are not known. That is troubling, and is something her family and friends may eventually accept.

Laura, Kurt, and I had been talking for some time. Laura decided to show me a series of photos she kept on her personal computer that were taken of Kristie when she had competed in a state high school girls sectional track meet. Laura described what was taking place in each photo. Kristie was in the pole vault pit just after she had cleared the bar at ten feet. If the bar stayed up, Kristie would qualify for the state tournament. Kristie was kneeling just after the vault, looking at the bar, and her facial expression said it all—"will the bar stay up?" Then, when she knew the bar would remain in place, a spontaneous look of Yes! and then elation. In the last photo, Kristie was being hugged by joyful friends and teammates. Kristie had qualified for the Illinois girls' state track meet.

I then found out from Kurt that there was more to the story. As a Deerfield High School student, Kristie did not have the natural strength to be good at pole vaulting, so Kristie did weight training with the boys to strengthen her upper and lower body. She lacked the speed of some of the other girls competing in the event, and speed is a very important element for success in pole vaulting. However, she was determined to make up for some of that lack of speed with excellent technique and a good work ethic that was combined with a burning desire to do well. She didn't place in the state meet, but just the fact that she had been able to compete at such a high level was an exciting milestone for a young girl who had wanted to step out of her comfort zone.

As a student at Boston College she majored in biology, especially liking chemistry and neurology. While a student, she did volunteer work at "the house," Suffolk County's House of Corrections. She also was a member of a volunteer group named 4Boston, a service organization at Boston College. At "the house," she tutored prisoners, helping them prepare for the GED test. For a busy science major to do volunteer work, especially for a young lady in a prison setting, would surely be a daunting task. Included in Kristie's writings were a couple of sentences that help to describe her thoughts about helping others: "I believe that the good we put out into the world is never wasted, never in vain. I think that even the most seemingly insignificant things change the world in their own small way"

The circumstances of her death were that on Monday, June 13, 2011, Kristie and a girlfriend ventured from the Chicago suburbs to downtown Chicago. There they met another girl and went to a concert in Millennium Park. While at the concert, Kristie and her friends began drinking. Kristie was two months shy of her twenty-first birthday. Included in her personal belongings returned to her parents after her death was the driver's license of one of her friends that indicated she was of drinking age, which is twenty-one in Illinois.

After the concert, she and her friend were planning to take an out-bound Metra commuter train on the Metra Milwaukee District North Line, leaving from Chicago's downtown Union Station to the suburban Deerfield Station, about twenty-four miles north of Union Station.

Kristie and her friend became separated before getting on their train when the friend waited for some food at McDonald's in Union Station, and Kristie went to the train to save a seat. There is video of Kristie getting on the 10:35 p.m. outbound train, number 2157. Kristie's girlfriend approached the 10:35 train, but became confused as to whether Kristie had boarded the train and chose to not board that train (the Union Station video records Kristie's friend considering and ultimately deciding to not board the train).

The Chicago Cubs had played that evening, and Wrigley Field was almost full, with over thirty-nine thousand in attendance. At game time, the temperature was sixty-three degrees, partly cloudy, with a very slight breeze. The game ended at about 9:30 p.m., and the train was crowded with those who had attended the game.

There was a witness who indicated that Kristie became sick on the train. Another witness indicated someone matching Kristie's description got off the train at about 10:52 p.m. at the Grayland Station, milepost 8.2, which is in Chicago, by Irving Park Road. The Grayland Station is a small and isolated station many miles from the Deerfield Station, which is a large suburban station located at milepost 24.2.

At about 12:55 a.m., an outbound Metra commuter train, number 2159, struck and fatally injured Kristie near the Edgebrook Station at milepost 11.6. The engineer operating the train saw what he at first thought was a pile of clothes on the tracks. It was Kristie lying on the tracks. A blood test taken after her death showed a high alcohol level.

Grayland Station. Wikipedia

There is only speculation as to why she detrained at the Grayland Station and eventually wound up on the tracks about three miles away. Kurt Topel believes his daughter was trying to walk home on the tracks. Kurt explained that this is not as far-fetched as it might seem. Kristie was known to "power through" logistical problems, evidenced by walks home from downtown Boston to her dorm at Boston College (in Chestnut Hill, more than six miles from downtown Boston). Kristie's phone had no power. While waiting at the McDonald's in Union Station, she asked her Deerfield friend if she could use her phone to alert her father to pick her up at the Deerfield station. Kurt feels that Kristie found herself alone and in what she believed to be an intimidating situation, and had no way to reach out for help. Knowing Kristie's inner strength, athletic ability, and social fear of strangers, walking home is something she very well might have attempted.

The Metra Milwaukee District North Line, between the Grayland and Edgebrook Stations, is a very active two track rail system. The 44.1 mile line has an average of eighty-seven daily train movements. Included in this number are about sixty commuter train movements, with the rest being freight and Amtrak. In the period from 2004 through 2012, there were twenty-five nonsuicide train accident deaths and seventeen train deaths ruled as suicides. (Wronski, Experts Seek Action to Cut Train Suicides 2014)

The track at Grayland Station is elevated and is about twenty feet above street grade, and remains elevated until beyond the Forest Glen Station. There is a sharp decline from the elevated tracks to street level, with little room for someone to walk on either side of the track bed. At Edgebrook Station, the track is at the same grade level as the street.

At one of the DRSC meetings, the Topels spoke of a conference they had recently attended in Europe that focused on ways to reduce the risk of certain types of railroad trespassing incidents. At the European conference, they obtained and brought to the DRSC meeting a hard rubber mat with a series of cones, appearing similar to upside-down ice cream cones, each cone about six inches high and placed next to one another, molded into the mat. If placed in strategic locations along the track, it could help keep trespassers off because the "antitrespassing grid" is next to impossible to walk on. Ed Sirovy, a founding and twenty-year member of the DRSC, and someone very knowledgeable in railroading, said that these types of devices had been used one hundred years ago to keep cattle off railroad tracks. Steve Laffey indicated that tracks in some western states currently have enhancements built into the track bed to keep wildlife off. There are locations along many of the Metra lines where these types of mats would reduce the risk of trespassing incidents.

The Topels also feel that Metra stations should be equipped with an emergency phone system so that a person in an emergency situation needing help has a way to reach out for it. I agree, and would go one step further in suggesting a video system also be in place.

Emergency alert systems both at the same highway rest stop on Interstate 55 in Illinois.

At first, there was a rush to judgment, and Kristie's death had been ruled a suicide, without any conversation with her parents or family. Kristie's father Kurt contacted the medical examiner and explained in detail what likely happened. The medical examiner changed the manner of death to "undetermined." With the help of Steve Laffey of the Illinois Commerce Commission and DRSC, the official records were updated to count Kristie's death as that of a trespasser. I asked the parents if any depositions had ever been taken of the train crew. They indicated that none had been taken, that they were grief stricken parents and did not think to inquire about that at the time.

The FRA database indicates that, in 2011, there were a total of 773 railroad trespass fatalities and injuries in the United States. Kristie Topel and the others are so much more than statistics.

Epilogue

· · ·

IN THE SUMMER OF 2011, I fulfilled a lifelong dream and visited the great state of Alaska for the first time. Traveling with me were my daughter Rebecca Swimmer, who had just graduated from Tufts veterinarian school, my teenage granddaughter, Bailey Rose Swimmer, and my teenage niece, Audrey Donaldson. We drove some fifteen hundred miles over a twelve-day period. Hopefully, I'll remember most of the details of this trip until the day I die. We drove from Anchorage to Seward, then to Homer, then back to Seward and on to Whittier. A ferry from Whittier to Valdez gave us about five hours on the water, then up to Denali, down through Wasilla and back to Anchorage before flying back home. Along the way we saw eagles, whales, moose, caribou, a wolf, and many other species of wildlife. The greenery, waterfalls, and snowcapped mountains only added to the allure of "the last frontier" and man's wondrous connection with nature.

Anyone who has had the good fortune to visit amazingly beautiful Alaska may have also visited the breathtaking Exit Glacier just outside of Seward. At Exit Glacier, like at many of the other wonders found in Alaska, the National Park Service provides tours. Our tour guide pointed to signposts that indicated various years from the past leading up to the glacier itself. She explained how each sign referred to where the ice field had been located in each of those years. Glaciers that took thousands of years to form are now slowly melting away.

My involvement in railroad safety started more than twenty years ago. During that time, I've met with and talked to many railroading experts. Many are more knowledgeable about railroading than I will ever be.

Steve Laffey, a thoughtful government official who is very involved in railroad safety, recently e-mailed responding to a concern I had. "One thing I have learned is that the industry moves at a glacial pace when it comes to adopting new technology," he wrote. I agree; we move far too slowly when it comes to improving rail safety. Just one example: it took years for the railroads to turn on a light switch so that ditch lights would make an approaching locomotive more recognizable. When it comes to proven and known ways of improving railroad safety, the railroad industry, local communities, and the federal government often move at a glacial pace in implementing change. But, like that little locomotive that could, persistence is paying off, and positive changes are taking place.

The one word that kept appearing in my research was "recommend." The experts, those in the know, would make various recommendations meant to improve safety, and the recommendations simply were not heeded, or were not heeded in a timely manner. The FRA recommended that the railroads start turning on the triangular pattern on their trains five years before they were required to do so. The FRA has long recommended that local communities become active in enforcing no trespassing ordinances and requiring fencing along the tracks. The NTSB recommended that the FRA establish certain requirements to reduce operator fatigue. Very experienced locomotive engineers and their union recommended that commuter trains be operated with two people in the front end. The FRA recommended that certain safety enhancements be established at existing quiet-zone crossings. When serious relay problems were discovered, the FRA recommended to railroads that the relays be inspected and either repaired or replaced. The FRA recommended that the crossings at or near commuter stations be modified to reduce the risk of second-train incidents. The experts know how to better manage risk. Unfortunately, their recommendations are too often ignored.

When designing a transportation system, in order to best manage risk, the importance of redundant, or backup, safeguards should not be overlooked. Redundancy, as it relates to safety, can be defined as the duplication of critical components or functions built into a system with the intention of increasing the reliability of the system. Both the FRA and the NTSB seem to ignore or minimize the importance of this concept.

The FRA has established certain specific choices of modifications that a grade crossing must undergo in order to qualify as a quiet-zone crossing. Some of the choices are median separation, four-quadrant gates, and changing the street to a one-way street and having the downed gate straddle the street. These choices fail to consider the additional warning time of about twenty seconds that had been provided by the train horn now silenced. The FRA knows that warning gates and signals occasionally malfunction and yet eliminated the redundant warning system of the train horn.

The NTSB indicated in four major incidents involving commuter trains reviewed in this book that the sole train operator—the locomotive engineer—had missed or misread the signal aspects, but the NTSB still did not recommend that two people be used in order to safely operate commuter trains. Experienced locomotive engineers testified that having two people operating trains is safer than having just one person—that four eyes are better than two.

As I write this epilogue in the spring of 2015, I am moved to know that, within the past several years, the BNSF has completed the installation of a four-quadrant gating system at the Monroe Street railroad crossing in Hinsdale, Illinois. My emotional involvement with railroad safety began as I was being rushed to the hospital just after young Jonathan Goers had been struck by a train at this crossing in 1989.

After the 1994 collision that took the life of his daughter, Lauren, and injured his son, Dr. Lanny Wilson said that he would see the day when a safer four-gate quadrant system was installed at the Monroe Street crossing. Now there will be one less predictable contributing factor leading up to a collision at that crossing. With the new system in place, it will be almost impossible for vehicles to go around downed gates. It is believed that this is the first four-quadrant gating system at a three-track rail line crossing in the United States. Hopefully, many more will soon follow.

Linda and Michael DeLarco wanted to improve rail safety after their son Michael's tragic collision at the River Grove Station crossing in 2004. They, too, are members of the DuPage Railroad Safety Council. It took years of effort on their part, but, eventually, the River Grove crossing was redesigned with the barrier warning gate extended to include both the pedestrian sidewalk and busy Thatcher Avenue. The station platform has been redesigned so that commuters are channeled to walk behind the downed gate barrier when trains are approaching.

The Wilson, Topel, Goers, Olivera, and DeLarco families, like many I have met through my long involvement in railroad safety, give profound meaning to words from the Talmud, "whoever saves a life, it is considered as if he saved an entire world."

In April 2012, the Federal Railroad Administration issued a publication entitled "Guidance on Pedestrian Crossing Safety at or Near Passenger Stations." The publication offers detailed and specific suggestions on how to make crossings near commuter stations safer. These suggestions include first-train and second-train visual and audible warnings when trains are approaching, channeling commuters behind warning gates, better signage, and better fencing.

On March 1, 2015 I posted the following in Facebook: "Yesterday evening a Metra/BNSF commuter train was stopped in the Main Street Station in Downers Grove and a freight train passed through the station and struck and killed a pedestrian. The Metra/BNSF is the only line of Metra's 11 lines that does not have a holdout instruction for their trains to obey and far too many accidents are occurring because of it."

Within a few seconds, I was deeply saddened to receive a response from my former nursing assistant class teacher and good friend Debby Manna-Hill that her son Jim Hill was the young man who was struck and killed.

BIBLIOGRAPHY

Administration, Federal Railroad. *FRA Notice of Safety Advisory 2000-1.* 2000. https://www.federalregister.gov/articles/2000/05/11/00-11866/notice-of-safety-advisory-2000-.

Administration, Federal Railroad. "FRA Oversight Plan for Northeast Illinois Regional Commuter Railroad." press release, 2013.

Associated Press. "Parade Where Vets Killed Used Route for 3 Years." November 10, 2012.

Associated Press. "Union Recommends 2 Workers in All Train Cabs." March 4, 2009.

Associated Press. "Union Recommends 2 Workers in All Train Cabs." March 4, 2009 .

Austin Peterson, Liz. "Astronaut Mourns His Mother from Space." *Desert News (Salt Lake City)*, December 21, 2007.

Biasco, Joseph. "Train wreck intersection has safety measures in place." *mywesttexas.com*, November 22, 2012.

Biasco, Paul. "$6 Million Settlement in Dance Teacher's Death." *Daily Herald*, March 14, 2012.

BNSF. *Federal Railroad Administration Railroad/Accident Incident #1111201.* FRA, 2011.

Board, National Transportation Safety. "DCA04MR001." accident report, documents, witness transcripts, 2002.

Board, National Transportation Safety. "Highway Accident Report HWY-06-MH-007." 2005.

Board, National Transportation Safety. "Highway/Railroad Accident Report NTSB/HAR-96/02, PB 96-916202." 1996, 29.

Board, National Transportation Safety. "NTSB Accident Report, NTSB/HAR -13/02, PB2014-100830, Notation 8462A." Midland, Texas Highway Accident Report, 2013.

Board, National Transportation Safety. "NTSB PB2002-916301, NTSB/RAR-02/01." Adopted 2002, 33.

Board, National Transportation Safety. "NTSB/RAR-05-03, PB2005-916303, Notation 7615A." 2005.

Board, National Transportation Safety. "PB2002-916301, NTSB/RAR-02/01." Adopted 2002.

Board, National Transportation Safety. "Railroad Accident Brief DCA-05-MR013, testimony, file documents ." 2005.

Bogdanich, Walt. "Death on the Tracks, A Crossing Crash Unreported and a Family Broken by Grief." *The New York Times*, July 12, 2004.

Bogdanich, Walt, Jenny Nordberg, Jo Craven McGinty, and Tom Totok. "Death on the Tracks: Questions Raised on Signals ar Rail Crossings." *The New York Times*, December 30, 2004.

Bogdanich, Walt, Jenny Nordberg, tom Torok, and Eric Koli. "In Deaths at Rail Crossings, Missing Evidence and Silence." *The New York Times*, July 11, 2004.

Bogdanich, Walt, Jenny Nordberg, Tom Torok, and Eric Koli. "In Deaths at Rail Crossings, Missing Evidence and Silence." *The New York Times*, July 11, 2004.

Boyle, Brian. "Freight train kills woman in Hinsdale." *The Doings*, November 27, 2003.

Carpenter, John, and Charles Nicodemus. "Noise Levels Citied at Crash Hearing, Padding Muffled Train's Whistle." *Chicago Sun-Times*, January 17, 1996.

Chicago Tribune. "Chicago's 21st Century Train Hub." June 17, 2003.

Chicago Tribune. "Metra train kills pedestrian, 70." December 17, 2005.

Chicago Tribune. "Oak Park bicyclist killed by Metra train." August 24, 2005.

Czeisler, Dr. Charles. *Fatigue Symposium Proceedings.* National Transportation Safety Board and NASA Ames Research Center, 1995, 60.

Daily Herald. "Scott D. Eskew." January 26, 2004.

Daily Herald, Arlington Heights, IL. "Engineer Follows Instincts, But Can't Stop in Time." January 18, 1996.

Delgado, Jennifer, Bridget Doyle, and George Knue. "Mom Killed, 2 Sons Hurt When Metra Train Hits Van." *Chicago Tribune*, October 17, 2012.

Department, Downers Grove Police. "Downers Grove Police Department Case #01-11-009122." Village of Downers Grove, 2011.

Department, Downers Grove Police. "Incident #01-6223." 2001.

Dinges, Dr. David. *Fatigue Symposium Proceedings*. National Transportation Safety Board and NASA Ames Research Center, 1995, 44.

Doggett, C. E. "letter to George Swimmer." September 27, 1994.

Downers Grove Police Dept. Incident No. 93-8038. "Downers Grove Police." Incident Report, 1993.

Drake, Joseph. "Pedestrian killed by speeding Metra train." *Downers Grove Reporter*, June 16, 1993.

Dungey, Diane, Jill Janov, and Ray Minor. "Noise in Bus Soundproofing May Have Muffled Train's Whistles." *Daily Herald*, January 18, 1996: 1996.

Editorial. "Congress, slow this train." *Chicago Tribune*, Ocotber 19, 2015.

—. "Slower trains aren't the answer." *Chicago Tribune*, March 15, 1997.

Eskew v. Burlington Northern & Santa Fe Ry. Co. 2011 IL APP(1st) 093450 (Illinois Appellate, 2011).

Fay, R. Read. "BNSF Superintendent." December 22, 2000.

Fe, Burlington Northern Santa. *Federal Railroad Administration Railroad/Incident No. CH0805202.* FRA, 2005.

Fe, Burlington Northern Santea. *Federal Railroad Administration Accident/Incident No. CH1205201.* FRA, 2005.

Federal Railroad Administration. February 2008, 2008. https://www.fra.dot.gov/eLib/details/L01500#p1_z5_gD_lEP.

Federal Railroad Administration. *Alerting Lights on Locomotives.* RR07-2007, U.S. Department of Transportation, 2007.

Federal Railroad Administration. *Success Factors in the Reduction of Highway-Rail Grade Crossing, Research Results.* RR-11-28, U.S. Department of Transportation, 2011.

Federal Railroad Administration, Office of Railroa Safety. *Guidance on Pedestrian Safety at or Near Passenger Station.* US Department of Transportation, 2012.

FRA Train Horn Rule Fact Sheet. Federal Railroad Administration, 2006.

Frankel, Todd C. "Report Pedestrian Rail Deaths Get Little Notice." *St. Louis Post-Dispatch*, December 23, 2012.

Gottesmann, Andrew. "Hinsdale School Copes with Car-Train Accident." *Chicago Tribune*, March 4, 1994.

Groark, Virginia. "Engineer tells of crashes: Metra vet at throttle in 2 recent accidents." *Chicago Tribune*, December 21, 2005.

Hall, Jim, interview by George Swimmer. *Chairman, National Transportation Safety Board* (March 12, 1997).

—. "Letter to Secretary Rodney Slater, U.S. Department of Transportation." Chairman, National Transportation Safety Board, June 1, 1999.

Hasvold, Larry, interview by George Swimmer. *Federal Railroad Administration, Chicago office* (April 6, 2001).

Heinzmann, David. 2000. "Crossing Near Deadly Train Wreck to Be Fixed." *Chicago Tribune*, October 5.

Hennessy-Fiske, Molly, Richard Connell, and Robert Lopez. "Witnesses Say Light Was Green Just Before Metrolink Train Crashed." *Los Angeles Times*, October 4, 2008.

Hilkevitch, Jon. "Violations Cited in Fatal Train Crash in University Park." *Chicago Tribune*, April 29, 2012.

"Illinois Administrative Code, Title 92: Transportation: Chapter III: Section 1535.502." n.d.

"Illinois Traffic Crash Report LOMB-3-20071219-161712, Agency crash report No. 07-52753." Police Department, Lombard, 2007.

Incident, Video of. Fairview Ave., Downers Grove, Illinois, August 26, 1991.

Janov, Jill, and Dan Rozek. "Investigation Likely to Take Months." *Daily Herald*, October 27, 1995.

Jimenez, Gilbert, and Mark Brown. "Probers Re-enacting Crash Today." *Chicago Sun-Times*, October 29, 1995.

Karlak, Pat. "NTSB Hearings Try to Sort Out Fatal Train Crash." *Daily Herald*, September 14, 1999.

—. "NTSB Hearings Try to Sort Out Fatal Train Crash." *Daily Herald*, September 14, 1999.

Kerrill, Tamara. "Deadly Crossings Plague State." *Sun Times*, October 26, 1995: 1995.

—. "Area's Train Crossings: 800 Crashes In 7 Years." *Sun-Times*, October 29, 1995.

Koppel, Nathan, and Miquel Bustillo. "Before Fatal Midland Train Crash, a Litany of Errors." *WSJ*, October 25, 2013.

Lively, Debbie. "Joliet Woman Killed in Downers Grove Train Accident." *The Downers Grove Bugle*, November 16, 2011.

Lopez, Robert J, and Rich Connell. "Final Report on Deadly Metrolink Crash Comes Down to Signal Color." *Los Angeles Times*, January 20, 2010.

Main, Frank. "Truck Driver Cleared in Fatal Wreck, Bourbonnais Crossing Gates Weren't Working Properly, Report Says." *Chicago Sun-Times*, February 3, 2002.

McCarthy, Kevin M. "Watch Your Step." *Downers Grove Reporter*, October 25, 1995.

McKinney, Dave. "10 signal complaints tallied in '95." *Daily Herald*, October 28, 1995.

—. "10 Signal Complaints Tallied in '95." *Daily Herald*, October 28, 1995.

Meeting, Metra Board. November 12, 2010. https://metrarail. com/content/dam/metra/documents/Board_Information/ November%20Minutes2010.pdf.

Metsch, Steve, and Guy Tridgell. "Railroads: Signals Weren't Working." *Chicago Sun-Times*, April 20, 2010.

Mogan, Dennis, interview by George Swimmer. *Former Director of Safety and Rules for Metra* (July 30, 2012).

"NTSB accident report DCA-02-FR-009, interviews, investigative documents." June 12, 2002.

NTSB Safety Alert SA-038, December 2014. 2015. *Railroad Signal Visibility (Conspicuity), Railroads should be aware that LED signals may mask light from incandescent signals.* Safety Alert, National Transportation Safety Board.

O'Connor, Phillip J. "Elmhurst Woman Dies Trying to Beat Train." *Chicago Sun Times*, October 26, 1994.

O'Connor, Phillip J., and Art Golab. "11 Killed in Last 3 Weeks on Metra Tracks." *Sun-Times*, July 21, 1994.

Peña, Dept. of Transportation Secretary Federico. *Fatigue Symposium Proceedings*. National Transportation Safety Board and NASA Ames Research Center, 1995.

Peterson, Eric. "St. Hubert to Retire Jersey of Child Killed by a Train." *Daily Herald*, November 12, 2004.

Peterson, Eric, and Ames Boykin. "Family Grieves for Little Michael; Metra Continues to Investigate Death." *Daily Herald*, February 26, 2004.

Pyke, Marni. "Investigations of Metra Engineers on Rise for 2014." *Daily Herald*, July 24, 2014.

—. "Solutions to Rail Safety Tricky but Worth It, Experts Say." *Daily Herald*, September 19, 2008.

—. "In Harm's Way." Daily Herald, December 19, 2012.

R.R., Burlington Northern. "Federal Railroad Administration Accident/Incident No. GT1405." 1991.

Railroad Safety Statistics-Annual Report 2009-Final. Federal Railroad Administration, 2011.

Rosekind, Dr. Mark. *Fatigue Symposium Proceedings.* National Transportation Safety Board and NASA Ames Research Center, 1995, 21.

Rozek, Dan, and Dave McKinney. "A Call to Test Nation's Crossings." *Chicago Tribune*, October 28, 1995.

Rwy, BNSF. "Federal Railroad Administration Accident/Incident ReportCH1103203." 2003.

Skertic, Mark. "Trucl in Amtrak crash hit gates: witness." *Chicago Sun-Times*, September 14, 1999.

Smith, Daniel C. "Associate Administrator of Safety, US Dept. of Transportation." *letter to Robert C. VanderClute, Association of American Railroads.* May 17, 2005.

Spak, Kara : Herrmann, Andrew. "We Are Very Proud of Her, Family Plan Memorial Service ......" *Chicago Sun-Times*, December 22, 2007.

Sudak, Stuart. "Woman killed by train was 'lgally blind'." *Downers Grove Reporter*, June 16, 1993.

Swimmer, George. "Horrible Day." *Chicago Tribune*, October 25, 1996.

—. "Lower Train Speeds Can Save Lives." *Chicago Tribune, Opinion/ Editorial Voice of the People*, August 15, 1997.

—. "Safety fences needed near railroads." *Chicago Tribune, Opinion/ Editorial. Voice of the People*, June 15, 1996.

Union Pacific Railroad. n.d. http://www.up.com/real_estate/roadx-ing/industry/horn_quiet/index.htm.

Walsh, Edward. "5 Die When Train Hits School Bus." *Chicago Tribune*, October 26, 1995.

—. "5 Die When Train Hits School Bus." *Washington Post*, October 26, 1995: 1995.

Washburn, Gary, Ray Gibson, and Andrew Martin. "U.S. 14 widening created a squeeze too tight for bus." *Chicago Tribune*, October 27, 1995.

Wikipedia. n.d.

Wilson, Lanny. "The Healthy Spiritual Journey." 2013.

Wisniewski, Mary, Chris Fusco, and Art Golab. "Metra's Overtime Express." *Chicago Sun-Times*, July 12, 2010.

Wozek, Duane, interview by NTSB accident invstigation interview. (June 14, 2002).

Wronski, Richard. "Feds Say Metra Safety 'an Area of Concern'." *Chciago Tribune*, October 16, 2014.

—. "Experts Seek Action to Cut Train Suicides." *Chicago Tribune*, August 26, 2014.

—. "Federal Agency Bolsters It Oversight of Metra." *Chicago Tribune*, August 14, 2003.

—. "Feds to Conduct Safety Assessment After 'Scary' ." *Chicago Tribune*, June 6, 2014.

—. "OSHA Tells Metra to Pay Whistle Blower $38,000." *Chicago Tribune*, April 24, 2013.

—. "Pedestrian Rail Alerts Updated." *Chicago Tribune*, February 28, 2011.

—. "State Watchdog Faults Metra for Falsifying Work Logs." *Chicago Tribune*, July 28, 2014.

Zemaitis, G.J. "Aspiring teacher helped the needy." *Chicago Tribune*, April 5, 2001.

Special Thanks

. . .

AMONG THE DRSC's EARLY MEMBERS were Dr. Lanny Wilson, an obstetrician and father of Lauren Wilson; Dennis Mogan, a former locomotive engineer who served as Metra's safety director; Tom Zapler of the Union Pacific Railroad; Brian Sweeney of then Burlington Northern Railroad; State Senator Bev Fawell, who was chairman of the Illinois Senate Transportation Committee (Bev, who always went out of her way to be nice to me, died in mid-2013); Carole Messana (Carole has also since passed away; her smile would always light up the room); Rose Humiston; Leo Ditewig; Ed Sirovy; Lourdes Beard; Ed Lysne; Bill Prescott; and Stacy Swimmer, my daughter; LaVern Nottlemann of Operation Lifesaver; James Bedell of the Naperville Police Department; concerned citizens; Ken Lanman of the Federal Railroad Administration; Jim Kveton, a young Elmhurst police patrol officer in 1994 who has since been promoted through the ranks to deputy chief; Patti Smith, a locomotive engineer for CSX, and eventually an inspector for the Federal Railroad Administration; Richard and Ellie Goers, concerned citizens whose son was involved in a train accident; Bernie Morris from the Illinois Commerce Commission railroad section; Paul Froehlich, then with the Illinois Secretary of State's office, and eventually elected as a state representative; George Graves, Downers Grove police chief;

Gus Holman of the Winfield Police Department; Debbie Hare, then with Amtrak; Rick Talerico, a Clarendon Hills police officer; Wayne Solomon, a locomotive engineer for the Chicago and North Western Railroad (purchased by the Union Pacific Railroad in April 1995), and a member of Operation Lifesaver; Judge Donald Hennessey of the circuit court; and others. Over the years, the DRSC has been very fortunate to have so many of its members and meeting attendees be such active participants, and many still continue their active participation: Dr. Barry Kaufman, well known in the Chicago area as a radio commentator and very active with Operation Lifesaver; Jim Speta; Michael and Linda DeLarco; Fred and Barbara Biederman, very active with Operation Lifesaver; Bob Meyer, with the Federal Railroad Administration (now retired); Scott Swimmer, my son; Carla Swimmer, my daughter-in-law; Cory Swimmer, my grandson; Steve Laffey, with the Illinois Commerce Commission railroad section; and Betty Olivera, whose eleven-year old nephew, Victor Olivera, was killed when he collided with a train while riding his bike. Thanks to Don Lindsey, a former locomotive engineer and a former union official with BLET, who met with me over lunch and answered many of my questions; Daniel Paul, who helped in editing this book; Michael Stead, with the Illinois Commerce Commission; Paul Piekarski, a union official with the BLET who always gave meaningful legislative updates; Brian Vercruysse of the Illinois Commerce Commission; Brian Krajewski, who as mayor of Downers Grove formed the Belmont Underpass Task Force; and Mayor Martin Tully, the current mayor of Downers Grove, for his efforts to improve rail safety; Liz Chaplin, a member of the DuPage County Board and an active member in the DRSC; Chairman Kirk Dillard, of the Board of Directors, Regional Transportation Authority and member of the Belmont Underpass Task Force; Patti Bellock, Illinois State Representative and member of the Belmont

Underpass Task Force; Rick Ginex, former Village Manager of Downers Grove who gave direction and focus to the Belmont Underpass Task Force; Michael J. Miller, for over 15 years my boss and compliance manager at Prudential, who continually stressed the importance of properly managing risk

To those I inadvertently missed, thank you.

GLOSSARY

AAR: Association of American Railroads

Ambient light: The light of the surrounding environment that is not caused by illumination supplied by the train.

Conspicuous lighting: Obvious to the eye and attracting attention.

BLET: Brotherhood of Locomotive Engineers and Trainmen. The rail labor union was established May 8, 1863, and has more than fifty-five thousand members.

DOT/AAR: All at-grade and grade separated crossings, both public and private, in the United States have been surveyed, and data about each has been recorded on inventory forms. Each crossing listed in the national inventory is assigned a unique identification number consisting of six numeric characters and an alphabetic character, for example: DOT/AAR 123456A.

DOT: United States Department of Transportation

DRSC: DuPage Railroad Safety Council is a citizen advocate safety group that was established in 1994.

FOIA: Freedom of Information Act is a law that gives you the right to access information from federal, state, and local governments and agencies. It is described as the law that keeps citizens in the know about their government.

FRA: Federal Railroad Administration

Hold out instructions: Special instructions that must be followed by train engineers using the Metra/NIRC and Metra/UP lines on how and when a train can safely enter or pass through a commuter station that is either occupied, has just been occupied, or is about to be occupied. The purpose of the instruction is to reduce risk to commuters and pedestrians.

Metra: The commuter rail system providing transportation to the Chicago region. It is made up of eleven separate rail lines, seven of which are owned by Metra and four of which are owned by other railroads who provide contracted services to Metra.

Metra/BNSF: Metra contracts for services with the BNSF Railroad to operate this Metra line. It is Metra's busiest route and is 37.5 miles to Chicago's western suburbs.

Metra/NIRC: Northeast Illinois Regional Commuter Railroad Corporation is a separate subsidiary of Metra. It is Metra's operating arm and operates seven Metra-owned lines. The seven lines are the Heritage Corridor, Metra Electric, Milwaukee North, Milwaukee West, North Central, Rock Island, and South West.

Metra/UP: Metra contracts for services with the Union Pacific to operate three lines: the North Line, the Northwest Line, and the West line.

mph: miles per hour. (Example formula to convert miles per hour to feet per second: 70 mph × 5,280 feet per mile = 369,600 feet per hour ÷ 3,600 seconds in an hour = 102.67 feet per second)

Party System: The National Transportation Safety Board investigates about 2,000 aviation accidents and incidents a year, and about 500 accidents in the other modes of transportation - rail, highway, marine and pipeline. With about 400 employees, the Board accomplishes this task by leveraging its resources. One way the Board does this is by designating other organizations or companies as parties to its investigations.

The NTSB designates other organizations or corporations as parties to the investigation. Other than the FAA, which by law is automatically designated a party, the NTSB has complete discretion over which organizations it designates as parties to the investigation. Only those organizations or corporations that can provide expertise to the investigation are granted party status and only those persons who can provide the Board with needed technical or specialized expertise are permitted to serve on the investigation; persons in legal or litigation positions are not allowed to be assigned to the investigation. All party members report to the NTSB.

Eventually, each investigative group chairman prepares a factual report and each of the parties in the group is asked to verify the accuracy of the report. The factual reports are placed in the public docket. http://www.ntsb.gov/investigations/process/Pages/default.aspx

Railroad trestle: A rigid frame used as a support, especially referring to bridges, composed of a number of short spans supported by such frames.

Redundancy: As it relates to safety, can be defined as the duplication of critical components or functions built into a system with the intention of increasing the reliability of the system.

Siding: In rail terminology, a low-speed track section distinct from a running line or a main line.

Signal aspect: The aspect is the visual appearance of the signal.

Signal bridge:

Signal indication: The meaning of the signal aspect.

Unfunded mandate: A statute that requires state or local governments to perform certain actions with no money provided for fulfilling the requirements.

About the Author

. . .

GEORGE SWIMMER IS A CERTIFIED public accountant (CPA) who received his Bachelor of Science degree from Northern Illinois University. A registered investment advisor, Swimmer holds various insurance licenses. He is also a certified nursing assistant (CNA).

An outspoken citizen advocate who spent over twenty years investigating train accidents and arguing for improved railroad safety, Swimmer is a recipient of the Citizen Advocacy Center's Citizen Initiative Award, the Lions Clubs International Foundation's Melvin Jones Fellow Award, and the DuPage Railroad Safety Council's Jonathan Goers Award.

A former member of the Belmont Underpass Task Force in Downers Grove. The Task Force successfully worked towards the completion of an underpass at the busy BNSF railroad tracks that cross Belmont Avenue. A former member of the Illinois Task Force on Fetal Alcohol Spectrum Disorders (FASD). The founder and former member of Illinois FACES, a foster parent advocacy group.

Swimmer also served as a member of the Marine Corps Active Reserves.

George Swimmer can be contacted at georgeswimmer1@gmail.com

Made in the USA
Lexington, KY
16 May 2017